TECHNICAL
SKILLS
for Alpine Skiing

Photography by Alan Schönberger

TECHNICAL SKILLS
for Alpine Skiing

by Ellen Post Foster

Published by the Turning Point Ski Foundation
P.O. Box 246, South Hero, VT 05486 U.S.A.

Copyright © 1995 by the Turning Point Ski Foundation
Completely Revised Edition, 1995
Printed in the United States of America by RR Donnelley
& Sons Company, Harrisonburg, Virginia.

Library of Congress Catalog Card Number: 95-90528
ISBN 0-9647390-2-X $15.95

Design by Alan Schönberger

Books available from the Turning Point Ski Foundation,
P.O. Box 943, Edwards, CO 81632
puppet@vailnet.org

During my years of coaching, I realized that it was most important for me to listen to the kids and to visualize skiing through their eyes. I came to understand that I had to learn from their responses, paying careful attention to what they said, how they interpreted my thoughts and demonstrations, and how they adapted their skiing. After all, it was the words spoken to me by a very young child that ultimately captured the attention of the ski world when he described a ski area as "my mountain playground."

Ellen Post Foster

Where Dreams Begin

AUTHOR'S NOTE

I wish to express heartfelt thanks to
Alan Schönberger
Emily Katz Anhalt
Frieda and Dan Post
Werner Schnydrig.
Without Alan's help, this work would have remained on my book shelf.
Emily, my skiing friend since childhood, carefully edited my writings
from the perspective of an English professor. My parents spent count-
less hours diligently helping me through technical revisions. Werner
shared invaluable knowledge and helped me throughout the writing of
this book. I would also like to thank Scott Nyman, Betty Gras, John
Peppler, and Carol Levine, who reviewed my work with care.

I am grateful
–to the outstanding young people who were photographed for the book.
–to Alan Henceroth and the Arapahoe Basin Ski Patrol who went out of
their way to help us in every way.
–to the Professional Ski Instructors of America Central and Rocky
Mountain divisions' Education Foundations for their support, and to
have the opportunity to share my knowledge as an instructor and coach
with the members of my profession.
–to Mike DeCesaro and Charlie Adams for their contribution on behalf
of *Skis Dynastar,* to Marc Hauser and Dennis Leedom of *Boeri* ski helmets, to Hank Tauber of *Marker* ski bindings, Lisa Wilcox of *Bolle* goggles, and Hugh Schure and Greg McCreery of *Phenix* skiwear.

Special thanks to Brad, Randi and Will Foster for their patience, under-
standing and smiles.

FOREWORD

Mike Porter
Director, Vail/Beaver Creek Ski School
Head Coach, PSIA National Demonstration Team

I worked with and coached Ellen Foster on the PSIA National
Demonstration Team for eight years. During this period, Ellen developed an excellent reputation for the content of her clinics, her innovative
exercises and her ability to develop a logical progression that produced
results. She has an excellent grasp of skiing fundamentals and an ability
to express them in a clear and concise manner.

In *Technical Skills for Alpine Skiing*, Ellen has incorporated into an
orderly, skills-based reference work all of the concepts that were the
foundation for her teaching successes. The result is an excellent book
for all people who coach or teach children.

The design of each chapter in *Technical Skills for Alpine Skiing* is very
innovative. Ellen develops the mechanical focus in a clear manner with
a broad list of exercises to achieve an outcome, and then, expands the
range of performance to include terrain, snow conditions and turn radius
variations. This is a complete book in that it provides all of the content
and strategies needed to meet the ever-changing challenges inherent in
our sport.

Perhaps the most important point is that Ellen's approach and exercises
are fun, exciting and encourage continued development.

Martin Olson
Technical Coordinator,
Canadian Ski Instructors' Alliance

Parents, coaches and instructors finally have a complete book to guide
them through successful development of young skiers. *Technical Skills
for Alpine Skiing* is an impressive collection of drills, exercises, and
games—and how to use them. In the section "Skiing Fundamentals,"
the easy to follow text takes the mystery out of ski technique. Applying
the method of skill development, photographs and logical layout lead
the reader through the stages from wedge tuns to expert skiing. Skill
development has proven itself as the most effective way to learn skiing
and is used by successful teachers and coaches around the world.

Technical Skills for Alpine Skiing is the result of years of practical experience by a gifted teacher. It will serve as a valuable resource and guide
for years to come.

Werner Schnydrig
Head Junior Development Coach,
Steamboat Springs Winter Sports Club

Versatility, spontaneity, and the ability to safely search for speed are all enhanced by developing a complete technical foundation. This is the basis for *Technical Skills for Alpine Skiing*. Ellen has learned from her coaching and teaching experiences that the main motivations for kids to ski are to have fun, to improve existing skills, or to learn new skills. With this in mind, this book was designed for athletes to have fun through self improvement.

My junior skiers have benefited tremendously as a result of including much of the material in *Technical Skills for Alpine Skiing* in their training for the past five years. The benefits derived from practicing these skills correctly helped increase the technical proficiency of my athletes. Not only are they much improved free-skiers, but they are consistently scoring top race results.

When Blaise Rastello, featured in this book's action photographs, was first introduced to this material, he was very receptive. He realized the value of learning to ski well in order to ski fast. After practicing the drills, Blaise was very excited as he told me he was skiing better than ever before. The following week, he won the Rocky Mountain JIV Championship.

Technical Skills for Alpine Skiing should be found stimulating and helpful by everyone involved in teaching and coaching children. And just as Ellen would hope for, the greatest beneficiaries of her efforts will be the children.

PREFACE

Ellen Post Foster

As a coach, I was continually looking for new ways to help each team member to improve his or her performance. The challenge for me was to discover new ways to present ideas and information, and new ways to organize my collection of skiing drills in order to meet most effectively the specific needs of each skier.

Much of the material for this book originated from my experiences with these young racers. It all began with the pieces of paper that filled my jacket pockets. These well-used papers were covered with exercise lines and specific drills aimed at overcoming individual weaknesses or building overall skills. Revising my plans and creating new directions, I saved the previous ones, and filled the pages of numerous notebooks. These notes became the basis for *Technical Skills for Alpine Skiing*.

In organizing my notes and shaping the book, I had several objectives in mind. Most important of all, I wanted to include take-to-the-snow information based on the development of well-rounded skiing skills. Since superb performance can only grow from a strong base, I realized that I needed to organize the exercises in a progression, building from wedge turns, in order to reach a high level of expertise. The book is, therefore, organized for systematic use so that specific information is readily available. I have always envisioned it as a resource book—a book comprised of pages well used and worn, that captures the essence of my old notebooks.

Although my old notebooks are filled entirely with written text, the words evoke, for me, very clear images derived from my actual experiences. Only a photo-filled book could represent my work effectively. The photographs are of young demonstrators "turning" the pages into a picture book that can be shared with all young skiers.

After finishing the text, I felt the book was still incomplete. The technical words were there, but the heart of my old notebooks was missing. This could only be expressed by sharing some of my experiences. The true stories preceding each chapter relate experiences that had a deep effect on my development as an instructor, a coach and as a person.

This book is dedicated to all of the kids who have skied into my life.

SYNOPSIS

DEMONSTRATORS:

Brett Buckles, age 13
Tony Cesolini, age 10
Cassidy Kurtz, age 10
David Lamb, age 11
Christopher Malato, age 12
Michael Nyman, age 14
Steven Nyman, age 13
Blaise Rastello, age 13

Ellen Post Foster

NARRATIVES

CONTENTS

CHARACTERISTICS OF TURNS

CHAPTER 3
WEDGE TURNS

BALANCING EXERCISES

SKILL DEVELOPMENT

SKI POLE ACTION

TURN SHAPE

TERRAIN/SNOW CONDITIONS

PERCEPTUAL SKILLS

CHAPTER 4
BEGINNING PARALLEL TURNS

BALANCING EXERCISES

SKILL DEVELOPMENT

SKILL DEVELOPMENT

SKI POLE ACTION

TURN SHAPE

TERRAIN/SNOW CONDITIONS

PERCEPTUAL SKILLS

CHAPTER 6
DYNAMIC TURNS – Short Radius

BALANCING EXERCISES

SKILL DEVELOPMENT

SKI POLE ACTION

TURN SHAPE

TERRAIN/SNOW CONDITIONS

PERCEPTUAL SKILLS

CHAPTER 7
STEP TURNS

A. PARALLEL STEP TURNS

BALANCING EXERCISES

SKILL DEVELOPMENT

B. CONVERGING STEP TURNS

BALANCING EXERCISES

SKILL DEVELOPMENT

C. DIVERGING STEP TURNS

BALANCING EXERCISES

SKILL DEVELOPMENT

GLOSSARY

APPENDIX
DOWNHILL TUCK

APPENDIX II
EQUIPMENT

AFTERWORD

CHAPTER 1
DIRECTED FREE SKIING

In Royal Company

I earned my first pair of skis by reading books. For each book that I read, my parents awarded a point. With the points that I accumulated, I could "buy" something I wanted. Since my brother wanted skis, I decided I needed to have them too. I'm not sure I really knew what they were at the time.

When I was older, my sister and I were allowed to spend our own money for ski school lessons. We could only do this after we had learned all that we had been taught in a previous lesson. After one of these lessons, the ski school director asked us to become members of the newly established Jiminy Peak Junior Demonstration Team.

From that day on, I felt as if I were in royal company. I looked upon all of the members of our team as kings and queens of the mountain. We turned right and left eagerly pursuing perfection as we attempted to master our skis and master the challenges of the mountain. We learned together by working hard, challenging each other, and helping each other.

Our Junior Demonstration team was part of a program called "Ski Masters." Ski Masters began at Mt. Cranmore, New Hampshire, in 1965 and became popular throughout New England. Ski school forms and classic exercises provided the foundation for our development. The forms, taken from the *American Ski Technique* of that time, were stem turns, stem christies, parallel christies and shortswing. We demonstrated these maneuvers at Ski Masters championships where we were judged on technique, symmetry of turns and consistency of speed. The skills we developed in order to master these forms are the same skills that are emphasized today. Free skiing runs were also part of the competition. While skiing the mountain, we were judged on how well we adapted to varying terrain in addition to the technical aspects of our turns.

As I moved on to other skiing challenges elsewhere, I was continually trying to recreate the spirit that seemed to ennoble us in those early days. Years later, I returned to Jiminy Peak. Although *Whirl Away* no longer appeared to be so steep, the perceptions I had about my childhood experiences never changed. I had learned to strive for improvement, to appreciate effort, and to value teamwork. With Tommy Tuggey, Marion Post, Jim Katz and many others, I shared disappointments, breakthroughs, determination and most of all, friendship. My childhood centered around the adventures and events that took place in the years we reigned. I gained a life-long love for skiing while I had the honor to be a member of that team.

CHAPTER 1
DIRECTED FREE SKIING

Technical Skills for Alpine Skiing is designed to teach school-age skiers to ski expertly. It is written to assist instructors, coaches, and parents in a way that will benefit young skiers. Most high school students and many younger students will be able to read and learn from the book directly. The material is organized progressively, and descriptions are concise and accompanied by explanatory photographs to help skiers become more knowledgeable. The material is presented either in a general context or as if spoken directly to the skier. By speaking directly, the material is more personal and easier to internalize. Although in application, particularly for very young skiers, instruction will come from the coach, instructor, or parent.

Over the past five years, the staff of the Steamboat Springs Winter Sports Club in Colorado has worked with much of the material that was assembled for this book. Head Junior Development Coach, Werner Schnydrig states, "The benefits derived from practicing these skills correctly helped increase the technical proficiency of my athletes dramatically. Not only are they much improved free-skiers, but they are consistently scoring top race results." In the last two years, one hundred percent of Werner's Junior III team qualified to compete in the Rocky Mountain Junior Olympic Championships.

Werner Schnydrig with J–V champion Tony Cesolini

Learning New Skills

Children possess a natural gliding ability that can be refined through skill development as their turns take shape. Their attitude toward movement has much to do with this gliding ability.

Consider children at a playground. They are constantly in motion—running, swinging, sliding, and spinning. A child on a swing wants to go higher. Another child flies down a slide and hits the ground running. Movement is fun and exciting. Typically, this attitude is brought into a child's first ski experience. Whereas an adult immediately wants to know how to stop, a child rarely asks that question.

Too often, round shaped turns are not sufficiently devel-

Learning new skills

oped before young skiers advance to difficult terrain. On easier slopes, a child may not see the necessity of turning. It is the speed, the wind in the face, that makes skiing exciting. But the development of turns at a slow speed on gentle terrain is just as important. It will prepare children for later challenges. Technical skills will allow children to ski where they desire at a comfortable speed.

As young skiers meet challenges and succeed, they realize a sense of accomplishment. They discover, experiment, develop skills, take responsibility and gain confidence through skiing.

Directed Free Skiing

Young skiers are highly motivated by their desire to free ski—ski anywhere on a mountain. They also respond eagerly to challenge and the opportunity for personal achievement. With *directed free skiing*, experiences become more meaningful and will lead to greater ability. The information contained in this book is intended to provide that direction. Through directed free skiing, skiers can work toward a goal, develop a routine to encourage optimum performance, and add constructive focus to each run down the mountain.

Directed free skiing

Mountain Playground

Skiers are challenged by acquiring and refining skills, and by applying their abilities to ever-changing terrain. The mountain is like a gigantic playground. It provides skiers with endless movement possibilities and places to explore. It takes a tremendous amount of time and experience to be able to adapt spontaneously to terrain and snow conditions.

Terrain features and changeable snow conditions make every run a new experience. This creates a sense of adventure that contributes greatly to the excitement young people have for skiing. Learning is fun in a playful environment. Encourage every opportunity for miles and miles of directed free skiing time.

The mountain playground

Personal Development

Skiers of all ages can learn to direct their attention toward specific elements of their technique and work toward self improvement. Taking an active role in personal development is an important aspect of directed free skiing.

On Saturday mornings, members of our team would arrive at the mountain eager to ski. But it was not until Saturday afternoon that they would begin to ski well— as well as they had the previous weekend. This presented a problem on race days when the first run began at ten o'clock.

A plan was devised to help each skier achieve his or her best turns quickly. The first step began on Sunday afternoons with team members skiing their technically best turns. Notes were taken as they described the characteristics of these turns. The notes provided a theme for each skier to review the following Saturday morning. As they free skied, their energy was directed toward accomplishing a task. The themes helped these young skiers perform well and feel comfortable on their skis right away.

Using directed free skiing, establish a routine to recoup your skills when you feel unbalanced. It is helpful to select a speed and turn size that feels best. Consider starting at a slow speed on gentle terrain. World Champion, Ingemar Stenmark, skied as slowly as he possibly could to warm-up while his competitors skied by him at race speeds. Stenmark believed it is more difficult to ski precisely at slow speeds, and by doing so, his turns would be more accurate when he increased his speed just before a race.

Keep a checklist of key elements that work best for you. The list may include feeling pressure along the inside of your foot to stay balanced on the outside ski, using wrist action to plant your pole, looking ahead, etc. Free ski with specific objectives in mind to improve your performance.

Drills to Develop Skills

My old notebooks are filled with penciled-in comments about methods for ensuring success. I had two major

Free ski with specific objectives

7

influences on my work: I learned from experience and from the young people I was coaching. Listed below are some thoughts to keep in mind when using the drills and progressions described on the following pages. These were very important to my young teachers.

Use drills to achieve technical goals

- Use drills and games for the purpose of achieving technical goals. Explain why a drill is being used and how it will be beneficial.
- Relate drills and progressions back to actual skiing situations.
- Make sure that the drills are appropriate for the ability and the maturity level of the skiers.
- Include adventure, challenge and excitement in each day.
- Provide ample practice time. This is essential for improvement.
- Encourage precision and accuracy in executing drills to maximize their effectiveness.
- Use the Skill/Drill/Hill Formula:
    Skill – what you want the skier to learn
    Drill – the situation you create to encourage learning
    Hill – the appropriate terrain for success

Overview

Technical Skills for Alpine Skiing consists of seven chapters.
    Chapter 1   Directed Free Skiing
    Chapter 2   Technique
    Chapter 3   Wedge Turns
    Chapter 4   Beginning Parallel Turns
    Chapter 5   Dynamic Turns – Medium/Long Radius
    Chapter 6   Dynamic Turns – Short Radius
    Chapter 7   Step Turns

Chapter 2, *Technique*, describes basic turn technique. It details how direction and speed may be altered most effectively, efficiently, and gracefully. A young skier can develop expert technique progressively, particularly when given correct direction by a coach, instructor, parent, or reference book. Chapter 2 is the most technical chapter in the book. It requires careful reading and concentration on details. This material is addressed first because it pertains to all efficient and precise turns, including wedge, parallel and racing turns. It may be helpful to review this material from time to time as you progress through the other chapters.

Chapters 3–7 are designed to teach and refine skills that are necessary for precise skiing. As skiers become proficient in these skills, they can venture to more challenging terrain. Increased skill development will allow ski racers to achieve greater success. A twelve-year-old racer once summed it up: "When I ski technically well, I ski FAST!" Chapters 3–7 are subdivided into six specific areas of development, featuring exercises and progressions. The subdivisions are:
- Balancing Exercises
- Skill Development
- Ski Pole Action
- Turn Shape
- Terrain/Snow Conditions
- Perceptual Skills

Tasks and situations in *Balancing Exercises* help skiers explore body positions ranging from efficient to extreme. These exercises challenge skiers to strive for stability while moving on an ever-changing surface.

Skill Development involves the refinement of edging movements, rotary movements and pressure control. These elements blend together in varying intensities to promote a smooth flow of energy from one turn to the next.

Ski Pole Action encompasses proper arm, hand and pole positions, as well as rhythm, timing and intensity of movements.

The segment entitled, *Turn Shape*, helps skiers develop smoothly linked turns. The shape and size of turns are considered as we explore rhythm, carving, skidding, and speed control.

In *Terrain/Snow Conditions*, skiers learn how to apply their skills in order to meet the challenges of varying terrain and snow conditions and to ski competently in the bumps. The selection of appropriate terrain is also discussed.

Sights, sounds, and tactile sensations all provide essential cues about terrain, snow conditions, speed, and distances. The development of *Perceptual Skills* involves observing and using these cues effectively. This section includes tasks that develop visual awareness and improve the ability to judge speeds and distances and to use imagery effectively.

Following the last chapter is a *Glossary* of terms to help you locate definitions easily. The first time that a word from the *Glossary* appears in the text, it is written in italics.

Appendix I provides information pertaining to downhill tuck positions. Since most young skiers have the desire to "drop into a tuck," or "tuck the flats," it is important to learn to tuck correctly and safely. *Appendix II* provides information pertaining to the appropriate equipment for young skiers. Leg alignment and canting are also covered.

CHAPTER 2
TECHNIQUE

Watch Me Closely

A young skier named Steve helped me to understand the importance of trying to meet the individual needs of each racer. Although he was only seven years old, he skied extraordinarily well but seemed quietly unhappy as he skied through a practice course again and again and listened to the advice of his coach. The first words I heard Steve say were, "Can I go now?" I asked him where he would like to go. He replied, "I've always wanted to start at one end of the mountain and ski every run."

As we left the race course to begin Steve's quest, I asked him what he had been practicing. I couldn't imagine his coach finding much fault in the way he skied. "Oh, the same things," he said, "keeping my hands in front, standing on my outside ski, bending my legs."—All of which he did superbly well, almost picture-perfect. I learned that little direction for improvement had been provided for him, and that he felt ashamed when he didn't understand technical explanations. He was often praised but seldom challenged.

Steve became my skiing companion. "Watch me closely," I told him as we worked our way across the mountain. He stayed "on my tails," following close behind. He followed my short radius turns for the length of a steep run, and then, long, sweeping turns on the next descent. On a groomed run, I abruptly varied the size of my turns—five short, four long, three short turns. I couldn't lose Steve, even if I had wanted to.

"Don't you ever fall?" Steve quietly asked me. "Yes," I replied, "watch me closely and one day, you'll see me fall." Steve and I were skiing alongside a race course when it happened. I "caught an edge" and went down momentarily. I wondered if Steve would tell the others when we joined our group. But in his quiet way, he smiled instead, and didn't say a word.

For years I'd hear someone behind me and, without looking, know it was Steve. As a student of a "year-round" school, Steve had two months off during the winter. On the days I couldn't ski with him, I prepared lesson plans that he kept in his pocket and read on the chairlift. He worked hard at perfecting and refining his form. When we did ski together, Steve would ask me to watch him closely and I would follow him down the mountain.

Years later, after earning many impressive race results, Steve became a coach. We spoke about "his" skiers. Steve told me, "I take them all over the mountain, to places they've never known. I give them things to work on and I work hard at finding ways to explain things so they understand." He smiled and, in his quiet way, added, "I tell them to watch me closely."

CHAPTER 2
TECHNIQUE

SKIING FUNDAMENTALS

Technique

Technique refers to the way in which a person performs the formal elements of skiing. Body position and ski position are taken into consideration in an assessment of technique. A skier's technique improves with the development and refinement of technical skills.

Wedge/Parallel Relationship

A wedge turn is the most rudimentary turn performed in skiing. The skills that are learned initially in wedge turns are necessary for all levels of parallel skiing. Wedge turns are the best indicator of a skier's ability to blend rotary, edging and pressure control movements in a balanced body position.

Notice how the body positions of both skiers are alike in the adjacent photograph. The primary difference is the positions of their left leg and ski. In relationship to the right ski, one left ski is angled in a wedge position and the other left ski is in a parallel position. Otherwise, the positions are the same. A skier's degree of proficiency in dynamic parallel turns is greatly enhanced by serious development of technical abilities at the wedge turn level.

Instructors and coaches can use wedge turns to identify and correct technical deficiencies that impede performance and progress. Improper technique is more noticeable in wedge turns since shortcomings become obvious while skiing at slow speeds. Apply any corrections that are made in the wedge position to parallel skiing.

Wedge turn

Parallel turn

CHARACTERISTICS OF TURNS

Overview

Although optimum technique is constantly evolving, there are characteristics that are common to all efficient and effective turns. The following characteristics are encountered in accurate and precise turns both in and out of a race course.

- Balanced Stance
- Dominant Outside Ski
- Carving
- Steering
- Angulated Position
- Countered Position
- Smooth Path
- Functional Movements
- Pole Action
- Turn Shape
- Speed

Balanced Stance

A balanced stance allows a skier to stand vertically. It is difficult to ski if you are sitting back, if your legs are rigid, if you are bent forward at the waist, or if your stance is too low. A balanced stance requires a fairly tall body position that is supported by the skeleton. A stance that is too low involves muscular exertion which quickly becomes tiresome. Slightly bend your ankles, knees, hips and spinal column. A straight, stiff back is not recommended. Instead, round your lower back slightly while tightening your stomach muscles gently. Bending forward at the hips is a common mistake. Bending forward weights the tips of the skis and restricts leg movements. Try the following exercises with your ski boots on. Incorporate a slight bending of your lower back, while keeping your weight balanced over your feet.

(a) Tighten your stomach muscles as hard as you can and then relax your muscles. Next, tighten your stomach muscles just enough so that you feel firm but not tense or stiff. You should be able to breathe comfortably as you feel your muscles work. Tightening your stomach muscles slightly will help you to round your lower back and to be more aware of upper body movements.

Balanced stance

16

(b) Stand straight, with your weight balanced over the center of your feet. Then bend slightly at the ankle, knee and hip joints, so that your straight back moves purely downward, i.e., without moving forward or backward. Now, pull in your stomach muscles, bend less at the hip joint and slightly round your lower back. Do not move your shoulders forward or backward. This sequence aligns your body into the recommended balanced stance.

(c) Compare bending forward at the hips with a relatively straight back to rounding your lower back. It is helpful to look in a mirror to see if your movements are correct.

(d) Have a partner place one hand on your lower back and the other hand on the front of the cuff of your boot. As you flex to a lower stance, press against both of your partner's hands. In this way, your center of mass moves directly up and down over the center of the ski as you bend and straighten.

(e) When you are in a balanced stance, you have the freedom to lift your whole ski off the snow. When you bend forward at the hips, your weight also goes forward and your leg movements become restricted. Only the tail of the ski can be lifted from this position. Test your body position to see if you can lift your whole ski while staying in balance over the center of your weighted foot.

Keep your arms in front of your body to help with balance. Also for balancing purposes, your hands should be positioned a few inches further apart than the width of your body. Look ahead to enhance balance and to see upcoming terrain and snow conditions. Stand with your feet comfortably apart in an *open stance* for balance and stability. This will also enable you to acquire an edge angle quickly. The sensory feedback you receive from the distribution of pressure on the bottom of your feet is very important for making adjustments to enhance balance. Pay attention to the feelings, or feedback ("feetback"), you get from your feet in order to control your skis.

The balance point on your foot is located at the back of your arch near the front of your heel. Typically, this is also the location of the center of pressure of the ski on the snow. It is the leverage point from which your ski is pressured and rotary movements are initiated. This body

Bending forward (improper body position)

Finding the proper body position

Bending forward restricts leg movements

In balance with ski lifted

17

mass load point provides the most efficient location for rotary movement to take place.

At the start of every turn, it is essential to pass through a centered (balanced) position. This critical part of turn initiation positions the skier for the rest of the turn. Use subtle movements to adjust weight forward to start the turn, in the center through the turn, and slightly back for the completion of the turn. This action originates from the balancing point. It allows pressure to move along the ski, keeping it from building too strongly at any one place. As a result, the ski travels forward through the arc of the turn without braking sideways.

Dominant Outside Ski

It is essential to balance on the outside ski in order to control the arc of a *carved* turn.

Balance on the outside ski

Imagine a block under the tip and tail of a ski. When you stand on this ski, your body weight presses the ski into an arc (*reverse camber*). When the ski is tipped on edge, that arc is pressed into the snow, making a turn. The outside ski of a turn must be weighted in order for it to bend and inscribe an arc in the snow.

On hard snow, the inside ski is placed lightly on the snow. It is in position to become the outside ski of the next turn. This transition occurs when weight is transferred at the start of the next turn.

Carved Turns

To understand *carved* turns, it is helpful to distinguish the term *carving* from other terms that describe ways to cross the surface of the snow.
- *Slide*–forward travel of a flat ski
- *Slip*–sideways travel of a flat ski
- *Pivot*–twisting of a flat ski without changing the skier's direction of travel
- *Skid*–sideways travel on an angulated ski. In a skidded turn, sliding, slipping and pivoting motions are combined to produce a change of direction of the skier.

In purely carved turns, every point along the length of the ski follows the same path along the arc of the turn and there is no skidding. Carving maintains the skier's speed, whereas skidding decreases speed. Pure carving

Carved turn

is accomplished by weighting and angulating the ski so that it bends into a circular arc. The edge of the ski moves along a corresponding circular arc to form a sharp curved track in the snow. The radius of the carved turn is determined by the amount of weight and degree of edge angle applied by the skier, and by the stiffness and sidecut of the ski.

Steering

In *steering*, an additional torque is applied by the leg to change the path of the ski from the path of pure carving. The torque causes a pivoting action, such that steering always adds a pivoting or skidding motion to the ski. The steering is applied to decrease the radius of an otherwise pure carved turn, that is, to make a tighter turn. The track is no longer a sharp impression of the angulated ski, but rather, it is a broader swath of disturbed snow caused by the skidding action. Some steering is usually needed at the beginning of a turn, while pure carving is desired for the remainder of the turn. In reality, however, pure carving is a perpetual goal whereas some degree of impure carving is actually achieved. When the term, carving, is used by most skiing professionals, they do not demand pure carving, but imply an acceptable (minimal) amount of skidding. Carving is used in that context in this manual, too.

It is better to steer the angulated skis at the onset of the turn and not merely pivot them. With pivoting, the skier's direction of travel does not change until the edge engages after the pivot. At that moment, the direction of travel changes abruptly, which generates a braking action on the original path. The flow, and the speed of the turn, is disrupted. In addition, the sideways momentum results in a skidded turn. With steering, the skis are simultaneously turned and tipped onto edges setting up for a smooth arc, with minimal skidding.

Angulated Position

Angulation means creating lateral angles in the body to enhance balance. Angulation shifts the center of mass of the body toward the center of a turn, thereby compensating for the unbalancing effect of centrifugal force. Angulation can occur in the knees and hips (in combination with flexing of these joints) and in the spinal column. In an angulated position, the upper body stays relatively vertical, with shoulders level, while the lower

Hip angulation

19

body (hip angulation) or the lower legs (knee angulation) are at a slant to the snow. Knee angulation is primarily used at slow speeds. A hip-angulated position is a stronger position because it depends on skeletal alignment from the foot to the hip for support. Hip angulation is used in higher speed turns and on steeper terrain. Usually, subtle knee-angulating movements are used to make minor adjustments in edging in hip-angulated turns.

Countered Position

In a countered position, the skier's outside hip is slightly back in relation to the inside hip in a turn. In contrast, a common mistake is turning first with the upper body, which advances the outside hip ahead of the inside one, and causes the tails of the skis to skid. Countering movements generally occur together with lateral angulation of the hip and spine. Together, a countered and hip-angulated stance inhibits the tails of the skis from skidding through the turn completion, and directs the upper body toward the upcoming turn.

Smooth Path

The transition between turns allows a skier to move smoothly from one turn to the next. There are two types of transitions, as illustrated. In both cases, the center of mass of the body moves along a continuous curvilinear path. The center of mass never darts sideways into a discontinuous (zig-zag) path. In both cases, the legs and skis move from one side of the center of mass to the other. The cross-over transition is used between more distant or longer radius turns. In this case, the weighted skis are flattened after the first turn and then angled onto the opposite edges. Minimal steering is used, and the skier's weight holds the ski firmly on the snow. The diagram shows the smooth paths of the center of mass and the skis. The transition from edge to edge is relatively slow, although the skier's speed can be very high. The skier's legs are extended in both turns, but obviously they are angulated to opposite sides. The body crosses over the skis during the transition and professionals call this a *cross-over* transition.

The *cross-under* transition is used between tight, closely linked turns. As a result of rebound at the end of one turn, skis are unweighted abruptly. In this momentarily unweighted transition period, the skier quickly extends

Knee angulation

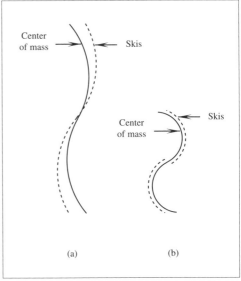

(a) Cross-over transition, (b) Cross-under transition

20

his/her legs toward the outside of the next turn to get on the opposite edges immediately. It is a dynamic, forceful action of the legs, while the center of mass of the body moves smoothly into the next turn. The legs quickly move laterally under the body, hence the name of the maneuver.

Before and after transition moves, it is always important to feel the inside edge of the outside foot/ski in order not to "lose" the edge grip and slip or skid sideways.

Functional Movement

Movements should be made with a purpose in mind. Unnecessary or excessive body movements often disturb balance.

Moving up and down, for example, should be done for a reason. Flex (move down) to absorb the pressure that builds through a turn, or to increase edge angle after the fall line. Extend (move up) to add pressure, keeping the ski pressed in an arc through the completion of high speed turns. Or, extend to flatten your skis at the start of a turn to make steering easier.

Unnecessary arm movements can interfere with balance and make it difficult to use ski poles effectively. In many instances, incorrect arm positions cause problems with balance and maneuvers. Often, underlying problems can be identified when skiers try to optimize their arm positions. Some of the common problems are listed below.

(a) arms held too high: lessens stability, encourages moving weight behind balance point
(b) arms held too low: encourages bending forward at the waist
(c) arms back: encourages moving weight back
(d) arm separation too narrow: inhibits lateral angulation and countered position
(e) arms spread too wide: inhibits pole swing, encourages body rotation
(f) outside arm too high: encourages leaning (*banking*) toward the inside of a turn
(g) inside arm too low: encourages leaning (*banking*) toward the inside of a turn
(h) arms crossing in front of the body: encourages rotation of the upper body, causes skidding of tails

Pole Action

At the completion of the turn, the upper body faces toward the mid-way point of the upcoming arc. The swing of the ski pole aids in directing the upper body into the next turn. The pole touch occurs during the edge change. These movements assist a strong flow of energy that characterizes linked, carved turns.

Turn Shape

Turns are shaped by the ability to guide the skis through round arcs. Round, completed turns allow skiers to ski with rhythm, and to flow through varied terrain without having to edge abruptly to control descent.

The basic mechanics involved in developing turn shapes are early weight transfer to the outside ski and steering both skis while progressively edging throughout the turn. The intensity of these movements can vary greatly. Although round-shaped turns provide the basis for all turns, these skills can be blended in different ways to develop turns with different shapes for distinct purposes. "C", "comma," and "J" shaped turns are described below.

(a) Establish the edge early in the turn and ride the edge around, drawing a "C" shape in the snow. This turn is very round, smooth and versatile for most situations. The roundness of the turn makes it very effective for hard snow and icy conditions. Pressure builds gradually and is not intensified at any specific point in the turn. Because of this, the edges stay engaged throughout the turn and are less apt to skid. This turn provides the foundation and is a prerequisite for all other turns.

(b) A "comma" shaped turn occurs when skis are redirected early in the turn. This requires a high edge angle and pressure very early in the turn. This turn is effective on very steep terrain where it is necessary to get the skis turned across the hill quickly to control speed. It minimizes the time spent in the fall line where speed can increase considerably.

The "comma" shaped turn is also characteristic of high speed turns that require a large change of direction, as can occur in race courses.

(c) A "J" shaped turn occurs when the skis stay in the

Pole action

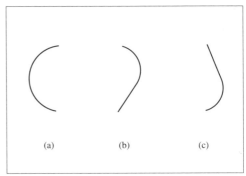

(a) "C" shape, (b) "comma" shape, (c) "J" shape turns

fall line longer and then rotary action is concentrated late in the turn. "J" turns are used in Slalom racing to maximize the time in the fall line (increasing speed) and minimize the time turning. The racer intensifies the rotary action into a small portion of the turn, getting on, and then off the edges quickly. Correct technique and precise timing make these turns effective.

The "J" turn is also effective in bump skiing where skiers accelerate in the troughs between bumps, and then control speed by turning sharply on the bumps.

A less accurate "J" shaped turn is typical for skiers who have not developed carving skills sufficiently to ski round shaped turns. Instead, rotary action happens with a quick pivot of the skis, and then the edges engage, resulting in skidded turns.

Speed

Ski racers must be versatile to adjust to any situation in order to maximize every opportunity to increase speed. They have to adapt to the demands of constantly changing terrain and snow conditions as well as a dictated course of descent (race course). The intensity, duration, and timing of their movements determine the size, shape, and speed of their turns. The following chart shows how the interplay of balance, rotary, edging, and pressure control skills maintain, decrease, or increase speed of travel. The same factors apply for recreational skiers, too.

Searching for speed

Factors	Decrease Speed	Maintain or Increase Speed
1. Turn Shape and Turn Completion	(a) sharper turn, shorter radius (b) arc interrupted by skidding (c) more completion	(a) shallower turn arc (b) carved arc (minimal skidding) (c) less completion
2. Edging	(a) skidded turn (b) more edge than necessary (c) hard edge at end of turn (d) staying on edge too long	(a) clean, carved turn (b) minimal edge angle (c) releasing the edge at end of turn
3. Weight Distribution	(a) weight too far forward, tails skid (b) weight too far back, tips skid	(a) weight centered over balance point

CHAPTER 3
WEDGE TURNS

Wedge Turns to Race Turns

There are two ways I remember Mike; as a seven-year-old determined to keep up, and as a member of the "Three Musketeers."

When Mike first came to our race program, he skied below the ability level of his teammates. He skied slowly in a wedge, unable to handle the same runs as the more experienced skiers. Right from the start, Mike always seemed to be chasing better skiers. As his skills improved, he looked for faster teammates to follow.

It wasn't until Mike met Geoff and Josh that he really found his place on the team. The three were inseparable, always challenging and chasing one another. They became known as the "Three Musketeers" as they explored the mountain in search of adventure.

The Three Musketeers became the nucleus of a young upcoming group full of determination and purpose. The name disappeared as three grew to four and then six teammates, all qualifying for the Junior Olympic Championships.

Looking through my old notebooks, I came across goal sheets filled out by team members at that time. One of the questions on the goal sheet asked what was liked best and least about skiing. Mike's answer to the second part of the question was left blank. I remember his coach saying, "There must be something you don't like." Mike smiled and shook his head. When the goal sheets were reviewed a month later, Mike was asked the same question. Mike smiled again as he gave his answer: "having to go back up the mountain; I'd rather always ski down."

Nine years later, the original "Three Musketeers" were still skiing together and full of adventure. Mike finished in the top five on the national points list earning him a Gold Pass to ski anywhere in Colorado.

My thoughts return to a seven-year-old, skiing in a wedge, unable to handle the easiest of runs.

CHAPTER 3
WEDGE TURNS

Wedge Turns are turns performed with the skis in a wedge position; the tips of the skis are close together and the tails are apart. Rhythmic, round-shaped turns are linked, maintaining a wedge of consistent width. Each turn starts with a slight rising motion combined with a steering of the skis into the turn. Weight is transferred gradually to the outside ski of the turn. The outside ski is tipped on edge; the degree of tipping (called the *edge angle*) is increased through the turn. The body is lowered by gradual flexing of the ankle, knee, and torso as each turn is completed. The upper body faces the direction of the upcoming turn.

BALANCING EXERCISES

Balanced Stance

A balanced stance is characterized by:
 (a) a fairly tall body position, supported by the skeleton
 (b) joints that are slightly flexed
 (c) feet that are comfortably apart
 (d) hands that are in front of the body
 (e) eyes that look ahead
 (f) balance on the feet at a point located at the back of the arch, in front of the heel; this is the *balance point*

Balanced stance

29

One Ski Scooter

This exercise is excellent for developing overall balance and for finding a centered stance. It is invaluable for learning to balance on the downhill ski of a traverse or the outside ski of a turn.

Take a ski off and walk around on one ski. Push off with your ski boot and glide on the ski. Scooter to a distant object on flat terrain. Scooter around objects such as ski poles, cones, or Slalom poles, to develop balance. After feeling comfortable on either ski, try to scooter without using your ski poles.

One ski scooter

Straight Run Exercise Routines

Perform the following straight run exercises in a balanced stance, gliding straight down a gentle slope:
 (a) touch your right boot top, touch your left boot top
 (b) march from foot to foot, gliding on one foot between each step
 (c) alternate sliding one ski forward as you pull the other foot back in a shuffling manner
 (d) lift one ski off of the snow (tip, tail or whole ski)
 (e) hop on one, jump on both skis
 (f) reach for the sky, touch the snow
 (g) side step to a new line
 (h) catch a ball and throw it back without using ski poles
 (i) duck under or jump over poles

It is fun and challenging to combine the tasks into different routines. Routines require concentration and they encourage practice time.

Lift one ski, touch the boot top

Balance and Movement Courses

Activity and experimentation in balance and movement courses can greatly improve the ability to balance on skis. Courses provide fun situations that help skiers develop their motor skills, increase body awareness, and improve visual awareness. On the course, skiers must look ahead to locate poles, cones, or other obstacles, just as they must look ahead when free-skiing or running gates. Balance and movement exercises also enhance edge control. Skiers move off the edge of one ski and then the other to change direction as they maneuver through a course. The experience gained by skiing these courses encourages balanced, automatic, and reflexive responses to on-snow challenges.

Course 1, Pole Step Over

Use ten bamboo poles to construct a course on flat terrain. Set the poles flat on the snow, pointing in random directions. Space the poles so that the ends are touching or up to two meters apart.

Step over every pole

Maneuver to step over every pole. In this exercise, practice transferring weight from ski to ski and balancing on one ski at a time.

Variations:
- Step over red poles only or over blue poles only.
- Follow a leader over all the poles.
- Hop over every pole, first on your right ski, then on your left ski, walking between poles.
- Advanced skiers can do the course later without using ski poles.

Course 2, Obstacle Course

Use twenty poles, or a combination of poles and cones, to set an obstacle course on terrain that is nearly flat but has a slight pitch. Use the poles and cones to create markers and obstacles that skiers move to, turn around, jump over, or ski under. An obstacle course can include the following activities:
(a) sidestep over poles that are lying on the ground
(b) circle a cone or a pole
(c) turn around and change direction of travel
(d) walk forward, walk backward
(e) pole across the hill
(f) jump over a pole on the snow
(g) duck under crossed poles

31

Use these activities in different combinations to design your own obstacle courses. Courses can be timed with skiers trying to better their results each time through the course.

Duck under and jump over poles

SKILL DEVELOPMENT

Wedge to a Stop

Ski in a narrow gliding wedge straight down a gentle slope. Maintain a balanced stance while keeping the width of the wedge consistent and narrow.

With a slight flexing motion, smoothly press the tails of your skis farther apart into a wider wedge. The ski tips stay close together as the tails of the skis spread apart. As the wedge becomes wider, the edge angle of the skis increases. Increasing the edge angle engages the edges of the skis against the snow, which slows the speed of descent. Increase the width of the wedge until you come to a complete stop.

The edge angle of the skis should increase gradually in order to come to a stop smoothly. In contrast, a quick move to a steeply edged ski can cause the ski to catch in the snow and bounce repeatedly or *chatter*, instead of holding.

Wedge to a stop

Straight Run/Wedge

Skiing straight down a gentle slope, alternate between straight run (in which skis are parallel) and wedge positions.

Flex and extend your ankles, knees and torso to make smooth transitions from parallel to wedge and back to parallel positions. Use a flexing motion in conjunction with spreading the tails of the skis into a wedge. As the skis move further away from the center of the body, the edge angle increases, slowing travel down the hill. Extend to flatten edges on the snow in order to pull skis back to a parallel position, increasing speed.

Balance should remain over the center of each foot. Focus on the feeling along the inside of your foot. The ski will be edged less when the foot is flatter. The more the knee and foot are tipped toward the inside, the steeper the angle of the edge will be on the snow.

Alternate wedge and parallel positions

Vary Wedge Width

Ski a series of wedge turns in a wide wedge. A wide position will result in braking and slowing speed. This is a necessary maneuver to learn in order to control speed on steeper terrain.

Compare wide wedge turns with a series of turns in a narrow wedge. Speed increases in a narrower stance since skis are tipped on edge to a lesser degree. A parallel stance can evolve from a narrow wedge when emphasis is placed on transferring weight to the *outside ski* of the turn combined with strong rotary movements (steering) of both legs.

Narrow wedge

Wide wedge

Turn Feet and Skis

In a narrow wedge, concentrate on the *rotary* movements of the legs by slightly turning your feet toward the left, then the right, etc. Your skis should be relatively flat on the snow in order to turn them. Aim your upper body down the hill to minimize upper body motion. These movements can be practiced first without skis.

Turn your feet and your skis

Edge Locks

From a gliding wedge, greatly increase the edge angle of one ski to move in the direction this *railed* ski tracks. Release the edge by decreasing the edge angle. Then, greatly increase the edge of the other ski to move in the direction it points. Use this exercise to feel *edging*, the engagement of the edge on the snow. An edge lock is an exaggerated maneuver in which more edge angle is used than is necessary to accomplish a turn. Practicing this exercise teaches the skier to optimize the edge angle instead of *over-edging* or *under-edging* the ski.

Increase the edge angle to lock the ski on edge

Outside Ski

Think of a turn as half of a circle. The ski that is closer to the center of the circle is the inside ski of the turn. The ski that is farther away from the center is the outside ski.

In a wedge, transfer your weight at the beginning of the turn to the outside ski. Reference can be made to a "heavy" and "light" ski in each turn. Verbal cues such as "right ski, left ski" to indicate weighting of the outside ski are often helpful.

Steering

Steering combines the rotary skill developed in *Turn Feet and Skis* and the edging skill developed in *Edge Locks*. It refers to the action of turning an edged ski. In a narrow wedge, rotate and tip the weighted outside foot/ski to develop steering. This results in a round shaped arc in which the outside ski travels forward through the arc of the turn, minimizing sideways drift or skid.

Steering; turning an edged ski

Foot Arcs

Pushing the ski away from the body to attain an edge is a common error. In order to develop an arc, the outside ski must be weighted, edged and turned. In this way, the ski travels forward through the arc of the turn. Sideways skidding is minimized, leaving clear arcs in the snow.

An exercise to illustrate the difference between these actions is illustrated in the accompanying photographs. Without skis, first push your foot sideways, increasing the edge angle. Then, inscribe an arc by simultaneously turning and edging your foot. Notice how the foot travels forward through the arc of this turn. Try to capture this feeling with skis in wedge turns.

Study Arcs

Study the arc that your outside ski leaves in the snow to determine your progress. Work toward a narrow rounded path in the snow and not a broad swath.

Flex and Extend

During the beginning of a wedge turn, slowly extend your legs. The extension helps to flatten your skis so they are easier to steer into the turn. When your upper body and skis face down the hill in the fall line, flex your legs to complete the turn. Flexing helps to increase the edge angle, continuing the turn. Flexing and extending discourage static and stiff body positions, promoting rhythm and linked turns.

Slipping sideways

Inscribing an arc

Upper Body Position

Excessive upper body movements or actions that compensate for weak lower body skills become more apparent with this exercise. If you suspect a problem, use this exercise as a visual tool while you develop correct movement patterns.

Loop one ski pole strap over the basket of the other pole. Then, place the ski poles around your hips and connect the other side. Make sure the poles are level. Ski a series of wedge turns and notice if the poles tip or turn, indicating:
  (a) leaning the upper body into the turn—poles on hips tip instead of staying level
  (b) turning the upper body—poles on hips start the turn before the skis turn
  (c) leaning and turning the upper body—poles on hips tip and turn

Upper body position

Turn Around Hoops

Set a course by laying hula hoops on the snow. Ski around the hoops, copying the smooth, round shape of the hoops.

Copy the round shape of hoops

SKI POLE ACTION

Arm Position

To be in a balanced position, place your arms in front of your body with a slight bend at your elbow. You can practice arm position with or without ski poles.

Explore Arm Movements

Refer to *Functional Movements*, Chapter 2 for a description of common problems that can result from incorrect arm movements. Try different arm positions to be aware of the effect they have on your balance.

Proper arm position

37

Pole Straps

It is important to use grips with straps for an effective pole swing and pole plant. To use properly, your hand goes up through the loop of the strap, and then down, gripping the strap and pole. Adjust the straps so they fit snugly around your gloves with your hand positioned at the top of the grip.

Pole strap position

Poling Across Flat Terrain

Initial use of the ski poles is for propulsion to glide across flat terrain. Plant your poles on both sides of your skis at a point in front of the bindings. Rock forward with your arms extended and then push down and back with your arms to slide forward.

Poling across flat terrain

TURN SHAPE

Drawing Turns

Draw smooth, round arcs in the snow. Show completed turns without straight lines connecting the turns. Turns should be *linked* so that the completion of one arc leads directly into the start of the next turn. Linked, round shaped turns allow skiers to control their speed smoothly without having to jam on their edges and skid in order to slow down.

Some skiers incorrectly depict turns as zig-zag in shape. This misunderstanding is often reflected in their turns which tend to be quickly pivoted from one direction to the other.

Draw linked, round shaped turns

38

Hand Turns

While standing or sitting, visualize turns using hand movements to represent skis. While holding your hands next to each other (pointed in a narrow wedge), turn and tip your "skis" from edge to edge through round shaped turns. Emphasize the outside "ski" of the turn.

Use hand movement to represent ski movement

Vary Turn Size

A larger, or *long radius turn*, requires a more gradual tipping of the skis on edge in comparison to the demands for a small, or *short radius turn*. Slow turning action of the leg/ski occurs in a long radius turn in contrast to the quick rotary action that is associated with a sharper turn.

Ski a long distance varying the size of your turns.

Control Speed

In a wedge, speed can be decreased by widening the wedge and/or by continuing to turn in an arc until the outside ski points across the hill before starting into the next turn. Speed can be increased by narrowing the wedge and/or by starting into the next turn *before* the outside ski points across the hill. In preparation for parallel skiing, controlling speed by the shape of turns is an important skill to learn.

On steeper terrain, it is necessary to finish the turn with skis pointing across the hill to control speed. At the moment of turn completion on flatter terrain, the skis point diagonally down the hill, carrying more speed.

Link turns with very round and completed arcs and then compare them to turns that are completed diagonally on the hill.

Lead-Follow

The leader determines the size, shape, and speed of the turns. Each follower tries to stay in the leader's tracks. When the technically better skier leads, the follower can focus on a specific movement to imitate, such as arm position. Or, skiers can predetermine specific movements on which they would like to be evaluated. They can take turns being the follower and providing feedback.

The follower skis in the leader's tracks

TERRAIN/SNOW CONDITIONS

Gentle Terrain

Terrain at this level should be primarily gentle, "green" runs. The greatest challenge for skiers of this ability is to learn basic skills and movement patterns. Difficult terrain provides an added variable that can lead to bad habits and be stressful.

Steeper Terrain

In areas where the hill becomes steeper, the edge angle on the outside ski of the turn must increase in order for the ski to grip the snow and not skid sideways. As the edge angle increases, the skier's center of mass moves slightly to the inside of the turn. The shoulders stay level.

Body position on steep terrain

Variable Terrain

Even the terrain on gentle slopes can be variable. Washboard-like rolls, side hills, changes in pitch, and gentle bumps need to be negotiated in order to ski smoothly down the hill. Terrain features provide an opportunity to explore movement patterns that enhance balance. These experiences will provide the foundation for adapting to abrupt changes on difficult terrain in the future.

To maintain balance over undulations in terrain, such as rolls and bumps, keep your upper body stable and use leg action to ride smoothly over terrain changes. Your upper body should travel a smooth path while your legs flex and extend to remain in contact with the irregular terrain. The bump should lift your skis underneath your upper body causing your joints to flex. Rock forward at the top of the bump to maintain balance while your skis descend quickly on the steep downward side of the bump. Extend your legs to keep your skis on the snow. Always, keep your hands in front of your body for balance.

Skiing over a bump

On side hill terrain, or fall-aways, the slope falls away to one side as well as down the hill. To avoid skidding sideways it is important to be balanced on the outside ski of the turn and to edge your ski sufficiently in order to grip the snow.

Side hill terrain

Hard Snow/Ice

On hard snow or ice, the skier's speed can increase quickly. To control speed, ski round-shaped turns and complete each turn with the outside ski pointing across the hill. Gradual tipping of the outside ski on its edge will develop a smooth arc. With abrupt edge movements, the ski will not grip the hard snow as well, resulting in chatter and sideways skidding.

Powder Snow

When you ski on a hard snow surface, it is primarily the edge of the ski that touches the snow. In powder conditions, however, skis often sink below the surface. When this happens, the entire base of the ski is supported by snow. The snow creates resistance as it is pushed away, causing the skier to descend at a slower speed. Dense, heavy snow (high moisture content) slows the skier to a greater degree than light powder (low moisture content).

It is very difficult to ski in a wedge position in deep, dense snow conditions. When one ski is weighted more than the other, it can sink and slow down, pulling the skier off-balance. If the snow is not too dense or deep, narrow your wedge, turn through a shallower arc, and/or ski slightly steeper terrain. Try small, shallow turns straight down the hill, transferring weight by pedaling from foot to foot. Weight the inside ski sufficiently so that it does not get pushed around by the snow.

Crud Snow

The expression, "crud snow" is often used to mean deep snow that has been cut up by ski tracks. This snow is inconsistent in depth and, therefore, difficult to ski. Balance is critical since skis accelerate abruptly as they enter areas where snow has been scraped away, and decelerate where it has been piled up. Seek the balance point under your foot to regain balance over the center of your skis.

PERCEPTUAL SKILLS

Visual Awareness of Objects

Visual awareness is necessary in order to avoid other skiers and potentially dangerous objects. Looking ahead and recognizing objects moves your focus down the hill instead of directly in front of your ski tips.

To develop perception of more distant objects, practice by looking for and counting objects on the hill, such as signs, blue jackets, or lift tower pads, etc.

Visual Awareness of Terrain

Absorbing and using visual cues effectively requires concentration, practice, and experience. Noticing and "reading" terrain is necessary for adapting to terrain changes.

Immediately after skiing a run, try to describe the terrain. Identify pitch, transitions from flat to steep or steep to flat slopes, side hills, rolls and bumps. Does the trail wind down the mountain, turning to the left or right?

Judging Speed

It is important to be able to determine how fast you are moving as well as the time and distance it takes to slow down. This is very important for safe skiing.

Set up tasks ahead of time, such as stopping at a given point on the hill, or stopping on a given turn—such as the tenth turn. These tasks require the ability to judge and adjust speed of descent.

Verbal Cues

Talking to yourself can help you emphasize an action. For example, saying "up, down" can promote movement, "left, right" can focus attention on the outside ski, and "turn, turn" can help you develop rhythm.

CHAPTER 4
BEGINNING PARALLEL TURNS

The Right Turn for Helen

Helen was the most timid member on our team. She was a beautifully elegant skier, but she lacked the confidence to ski aggressively.

Helen's turns were much stronger in one direction than the other. She was convinced that her race times would improve when her right turns matched the perfection of her left turns. But for a short while, skiing fast was not the only goal for Helen and her teammates. They were preparing for an evaluation test which would determine their readiness to race in a Downhill event.

Helen's group was caught up in qualifying for the race. There were strict rules, and they knew the staff was very selective solely for the purpose of safety. The requirements included the ability to maintain absolute balance on the outside ski, keep both hands forward at all times, perform safety stops, and follow directions.

Helen became very focused as she improved her weaker turns until she could stay on her outside ski throughout every turn. Her teammates sensed how important this was to Helen. They knew her participation in the race was not assured, and they rallied behind her, encouraging her efforts to qualify.

When Helen did qualify, I was surprised to hear her say, "I don't feel ready to go fast this year. I'll be ready for the Downhill next year." She always spoke softly, but this time her voice was full of determination. I was even more surprised by the reaction of her teammates. They immediately understood her decision not to race, and they respected her feelings. There was an air of admiration for Helen's personal triumph. Regardless of the race, she had succeeded in perfecting her right turns.

Once her decision was made, a change came over Helen. She became more aware of her own performance and she focused on self improvement in a way she never had before. It was the learning that became important and she treasured every opportunity.

Over the season, Helen's light touch on the snow became more purposeful. The graceful flow of her movements became more directed. And when she put her skis away in the springtime, she took her newfound confidence and carried it into her life.

BEGINNING PARALLEL TURNS

In beginning parallel turns, skis are apart in an open stance for balance and stability. At the start of each turn, weight is transferred to the outside ski as it is tipped on edge and both skis are steered into the turn. Edging is increased as the outside ski controls the arc of the turn. The inside leg/ski is steered to complement the movements of the outside ski. At the completion of the turn, the skier's upper body faces toward the mid-way point of the next turn arc. The pole swing coincides with the extension, directing the body into the turn. The pole touch occurs with the edge change.

BALANCING EXERCISES

Straight Run Exercises on One Ski

Perform the following straight run exercises while gliding straight down a gentle slope on one ski, and then on the other ski. At some ski areas, permission to ski on one ski must first be obtained from the ski area management.

(a) rock forward, rock backward, find the centered position
(b) hop lifting the tip, tail or the whole ski
(c) reach for the sky, touch the snow
(d) duck under or jump over poles
(e) swing the free leg forward and backward
(f) clap hands (without ski poles)
(g) catch a ball and throw it back (without ski poles)

Reach up, touch the snow, swing the leg forward

Side Step Over Pole

In linked turns, weight is transferred from the outside ski of one turn to the outside ski of the next turn. Side stepping is a balancing exercise that can help to develop weight transfer.

Stand beside a ski pole or a Slalom pole laid on the snow. Step over the pole with the ski that is closest to the pole. Touch the ski on the snow momentarily before bringing it back to its original place. Cross this ski back and forth over the pole.

Side step over pole

Terrain Garden

Many ski areas have terrain gardens with features such as rolls, bumps, pedal bumps, drop-offs, compressions, ridges, banked turns and jumps. These terrain features prepare you for natural challenges that you may confront while skiing on the mountain. Man-made terrain gardens are usually found on gentle slopes, so they provide excellent conditions for practice. The balance exercises below will be difficult for the beginning skier, but they should be mastered over a period of time to progress to expert skiing ability.

Refer to *Variable Terrain,* Chapter 3 for skiing over rolls and bumps. Pedal bumps consist of two rows of bumps over which one foot is on top of a bump while the other foot is down in a trough. These features in a terrain garden may be very uneven and abrupt. Try to keep your upper body traveling along a smooth path down the hill, while your legs flex and extend to absorb pressure and remain in contact with the snow.

A drop-off is a region where the slope drops away at a steep angle. It is important to anticipate this change in pitch by rocking forward. In this way, your upper body will move down the hill and not be left back as your skis accelerate down the steep slope. Focus on staying balanced over the center of your skis.

Terrain Garden

A compression zone is the transition curve between a very steep slope and much flatter terrain. When you enter the transition, your skis tend to slow down abruptly causing a concentration of downward and forward pressure on your body. It is important to enter a compression in a fairly tall stance so you can absorb the pressure by flexing your joints. Enter the compression with your weight slightly back since the abrupt change of speed will tend to lurch your body forward.

A ridge is a narrow path where both sides of the ridge fall away steeply. To ski along a ridge, turn on the sides of the ridge. The transition between turns (completion of one turn and start of the next turn) occurs at the top of the ridge. Turning on the side of a ridge is the same as turning on a side hill. Since the sides of a ridge can be very steep, it is necessary to weight and edge the outside ski of the turn in order to grip the snow. Change edges at the top of the ridge in preparation for the new turn. Rock forward to stay balanced while descending on the other side; extend your legs to keep your skis on the snow.

Skiing a banked turn

Skiing a banked turn feels very different from skiing on a side hill. Instead of the hill falling away to the side, it raises upwards and supports your skis. You can lean or bank toward the center of the turn since less edge is necessary to grip the snow. With skis flatter on the snow surface, your weight can be more evenly distributed between both skis, although the outside ski should still control the arc of the turn. Focus on guiding both ski through the turn.

To jump safely, it is essential to look ahead to the landing and ensure that it is clear of people and obstacles. Take off in a balanced position with ankles and knees flexed, and ready to spring. Extend your legs to lift off of the jump in an upward and forward direction. Hold your hands in front of your body for stability. For the landing, a fairly tall stance is important so that your legs can bend to absorb the impact.

Jumping

SKILL DEVELOPMENT

Side Step Shadow Chase

This game develops weight transfer and edging skills. Partners face each other on flat or gentle terrain. The leader takes single or multiple steps sideways changing direction often. The follower tries to keep up, copying the steps.

Side step shadow chase

Use the uphill edge of your downhill ski to provide a platform from which you can step up the hill. Step down the hill onto an edged ski so the ski does not slip. Move quickly from ski to ski.

The Side Step Shadow Chase is also a good warm-up exercise to start the day or to get moving after a cold chairlift ride.

Traverse

A traverse provides the experience of gliding across the hill in a parallel ski relationship.

Traverse

Travel across the hill, with both skis tipped onto their uphill edges. Keep more of your weight on your downhill ski. Each ski should track and not slip or skid sideways, losing the edge. Stand in a balanced, vertical position with the uphill ski and the uphill side of the body slightly ahead.

Traverse Exercises

Practice traversing on the downhill ski while tapping the uphill ski lightly on the snow. Increase the length of time that you hold the uphill ski off the snow until you can traverse across the hill on one ski.

The tasks that are described under *Straight Run Exercises,* Chapter 3 provide further challenges to improve balance and edge control.

Lift the uphill ski

Traverse Target

Use a ski pole or a Slalom pole as a target to aim toward in traverse exercises. The point at which your traverse finishes in relation to this reference point will provide an indication of how well your skis tracked on edges. Finishing below the pole may indicate slipping down the hill, which means a greater edge angle is needed in order for the skis to hold.

Traverse toward a target

Sideslip

In a sideslip, the skier slips sideways down the hill with his/her skis pointing across the hill. This is another exercise to explore edging movements.

Stand with skis tipped on uphill edges in a traverse position. Turn your head to look down the hill toward your direction of travel. Extend to flatten your skis in order to slip sideways down the hill. Flex slightly, moving your knees uphill, to edge sufficiently in order to control your speed of descent. To come to a stop, flex more to increase the edge angle on the snow surface.

Use this exercise to explore degrees of edging. The flatter your skis are on the surface of the snow, the faster you will descend. As the edge angle increases, speed will diminish or stop.

The sideslip also provides an indicator for fore/aft balance. When balanced on the center of the ski, the skier should slip directly down the hill without forward or rearward motion.

Sideslip

53

Forward Sideslip

From a moving traverse, extend to reduce the edge angle in order to slip sideways while traveling forward. A diagonal path down the hill will result. Explore the whole range between pure traverse and pure sideslip.

Boot Skiing

Without skis, work on the turning action of both feet from a parallel stance. For skiers who are at the stage that they use a wedge during the start of the turn, boot skiing and the following exercises will help develop a parallel stance throughout the turn.

Boot skiing

Pivot Slip

The pivot slip promotes a parallel turn entry and develops strong rotary movements of both legs underneath a stable upper body at the start of the turn.

Stand in a traverse position. Turn your upper body to face down the hill. Plant your downhill pole in the fall line and move your upper body down the hill. This will flatten your skis so they are easier to turn. Pivot both skis 180 degrees to a sideslip. Pivot around your ski pole, ending the pivot downhill of the point where the pole was planted. Finish in a lower stance to increase the edge angle and control the sideslip. Link pivot slips in both directions.

The pivot slip can also be used to develop round turns by slowing the pivoting action and increasing the edge angle. Steering into the turn will result.

The pivot slip is also a beneficial exercise for introducing the pole plant.

Pivot slip

54

Safety Stop

A safety stop is an essential maneuver to learn in order to stop and avoid obstacles.

Start from a tall stance, sliding straight down the hill. Quickly drop to a lower position as you pivot your skis to a sideslip position. The rapid downward body movement momentarily lightens your skis so they are easier to pivot. Turn your legs only, keeping your upper body facing down the hill throughout the maneuver. Increase the edge angle of your skis to slow down and come to a stop.

Hockey Stop

The hockey stop is similar to the safety stop but it does not have a long sideslip, or slowing down phase. It happens very abruptly and therefore cannot be performed at high speeds.

From a tall stance in a straight run, quickly drop to a lower stance to pivot your skis beneath your upper body, coming to a stop quickly.

A rounded turn completion can be developed by slowing the pivoting action while increasing the edge angle throughout the finish of the turn.

Garland Turn Entry

Garlands can be used for the repetitive practice of steering the skis down the hill, into the fall line. In a garland, the skis are first directed across the hill, then down the hill, and then out of the fall line in the original direction of travel. Linked garlands bring the skier across and down the hill.

Emphasis should be placed on transferring weight to the outside ski of the turn as both skis are steered (simultaneously turned and tipped) down the hill.

Garland Turn Completion

Garlands can also be used to develop better edge control and minimize skidding at the completion of the turn. Emphasize balancing on the outside ski and flexing to increase edging.

Hockey stop

Lift the Inside Ski

The outside ski controls the arc of each turn. To improve balance on the outside ski, try lifting the inside ski off the snow.

Experiment with fore/aft balance by lifting only the tail of the inside ski. Your weight will move forward toward your ski tip. Then make some turns lifting only the tip of the ski off the snow. Your weight will move back, toward your ski tail. Finish with turns in a centered position, lifting your whole ski off the snow Experiment with lifting the inside ski high, and then just high enough to clear the snow. Afterwards, place your inside ski on the snow so that it feels as light as a feather on the snow as your outside ski controls the arc of your turns.

Lift the tail

Lift the tip

Lift the whole ski

Inside ski on the snow

Jump Turn Entry

When a skier is off-balance at the beginning of a turn, it is difficult to complete the turn successfully. Jumping to start a turn encourages a balanced position. This exercise also exaggerates leg extension, and helps to develop a parallel ski relationship at the start of the turn.

First, jump in ski boots without skis. Bend your ankles, knees, and torso, and then spring upward. Try jumping as high as you can. Then, jump only high enough to clear the snow. Next, add your skis and jump from a standstill. If your weight is too far forward, it is difficult to jump and only your ski tails will come off the snow. If your weight is too far back, only your ski tips will come off the snow. Jump from a centered stance to raise the skis fully off the snow.

Jump to start a turn

Try jumping at the beginning of your turns. You need to be in balance at the completion of the previous turn in order to jump your skis off the snow.

Jumping is an exaggerated form of body extension. Replace this movement with a smooth, gradual extension of your legs to begin the turn. The extension flattens your skis on the snow, making them easier to steer. As you extend, feel the inside edge of your outside ski in order to control the arc of your turns.

Bobbing

When your legs are stiff, your skis tend to skid sideways instead of *carve* a precise arc through the snow. Bobbing develops flexing movements of the legs which absorb the excess pressure that can build on your skis through the completion of the turn. Flexing on an incline slope also increases the edge angle, continuing the turn.

Bobbing up and down

Practice bending your ankles and knees by bobbing up and down. Slowly extend to begin each turn. When your skis point down the hill, start bobbing. Continue the bobbing action until your turn is completed. Experiment moving slowly and smoothly in comparison to bobbing quickly. As you flex, balance on the inside edge of your outside ski in order to control the arc of your turns.

Instead of multiple bobs during the turn completion, slowly bob so that one downward motion occurs during the second half of the turn. By extending your knees and ankles to begin a turn, and flexing to complete the turn, you can develop smooth, round shaped arcs.

Skating on Flat Terrain

Skating promotes the transfer of weight from one ski to the other, and the development of a secure edge.

Push off an angled, edged ski and glide onto the other ski. After pushing with one ski, bring it parallel to the other ski before the next skating step. Repetitive skating with the same foot pushing off makes skating easier to learn. Remember to bring your skis together to glide between skating push-offs.

SKI POLE ACTION

Static Exercise

From a balanced stance, practice pole swing and touch primarily using wrist movement. Only minimal arm movements are necessary to swing the pole. Focus on swinging the tip forward rather than moving your whole arm.

Touch/Plant

Explore the intensities of touching your pole lightly and planting it hard. A light pole touch promotes the timing and rhythm of turns. Pole contact that is too hard can disrupt the flow of movement from one turn to the next. But in situations such as skiing through bumps, a hard, or very deliberate pole plant is helpful for stabilizing the upper body.

Pole Swing

While sliding straight down a gentle hill, practice your pole swing and touch. After touching the pole to the snow, roll your hand downward to keep your hand in front of your body while pivoting the pole off the snow.

Skating

Swing the pole tip forward

Turning

For first attempts, pole usage may mean touching your pole and turning around it. With experience, the pole swing occurs simultaneously with the extension of your body at the start of a turn. The pole touches the snow at the moment of edge change.

Pole swing

TURN SHAPE

Skidding/Carving

Contrast skidded, zig-zag shaped turns with round and completed carved turns. In carved turns, the ski travels forward through the arc of the turn and the tails of the skis follow the line of the tips. In skidded turns, the ski slides forward and sideways down the hill.

Skidded turn

Carved turn

59

Vary Size

Explore small, medium and large sized turns. Practice maintaining a consistent turn size, rhythm and speed, and also practice changing the turn size, rhythm and speed.

Control Speed

Ski round shaped turns on steep terrain, completing each turn with skis pointing across the hill, perpendicular to the fall line. Use completed turns to control speed instead of pivoting skis sideways and skidding.

TERRAIN/SNOW CONDITIONS

Easiest Terrain

Learning new skills should take place on easiest, "green" runs.

More Difficult Terrain

As your ability improves, more difficult, "blue" terrain can be explored. If the challenge of the terrain inhibits performance or progress, return to easier terrain.

Small Bumps

Turning on small bumps can help develop the rotary action of both legs and improve the parallel turn entry. In a field of bumps, the uphill part (top) of each bump provides the flattest terrain. The downhill part of each bump slants steeply downward. Control your speed by turning sharply on the top of the bump. Plant your pole straight down the hill for stability and to direct your upper body down the hill. Rock forward and turn both skis at the same time. Your forward commitment will allow you to stay balanced over your skis as they quickly descend the steep downslope of the bump. Press your ski tips down to maintain contact with the surface of the snow. Although both skis are turned simultaneously, weight and edge the downhill ski sufficiently to hold on the steep downhill side of the bump.

Skiing bumps

A common problem that occurs at this level is caused by keeping the planted pole in the snow too long. When this happens, the inside hand gets left behind, twisting the skier's upper body away from the direction of travel (down the hill). It also causes the skier to lean uphill making it difficult to start into the next turn. To avoid this, roll your hand downward following the pole plant in order to keep your hand in front of your body and stay in balance.

Long Turns in Bumps

Skiing medium to long radius turns in small bumps improves balance and leg movement. Try to maintain ski/snow contact, to keep the arc round, to absorb with your legs, and to keep your upper body quiet.

Terrain Features

Look for rolling terrain, side hills and knolls to apply newly acquired skills.

Hard Snow/Ice

Smooth, round-shaped arcs are appropriate for hard snow and ice conditions (see *Hard Snow/Ice*, Chapter 3). Slightly widen your stance on ice in case your edges do not hold. In a wider stance, your ski will slip sideways until the edge angle is sufficient to grip the snow. If you start in a narrow stance, the ski has much farther to slip before the edge engages. By then, the ski's momentum will usually cause the slipping to continue regardless of the edge angle.

Deep Snow

When a few inches of snow have fallen on top of a solid base, weighting the outside ski to control the arc of the turn is still effective. But as snow deepens, the skier's weight should be more equally distributed. If one ski is weighted more than the other, it will sink and slow down, pulling the skier off-balance. A narrow stance helps to keep weight distributed on both skis. Although both skis are turned at the same time, the skier's legs should remain independent in their ability to flex and extend for balancing purposes.

Skiing deep snow

The first turns are usually the hardest. Aim straight down the hill to gain enough speed in order to begin turning. Focus on rotary action of the lower body, turning both ski tips from side-to-side. Start with shallow arcs in the fall line, and then round out the turns as speed increases. Establish a rhythm to enhance movement from one turn to the next.

Skis are difficult to turn below the surface of the snow. In deep snow, it is easier to turn when the skis are close to the surface, on top of the snow, or in the air. Skiers can use flexion and extension movements to jump their skis out of the snow. Review *Jump Turn Entry* under *Skill Development* in this chapter. Active extension movements lighten the skis so that they are easier to turn.

At the completion of a turn in soft snow, the ski can bend in a deeper arc than usual. When the skier extends in the direction of the next turn, the pressure that bends the ski is released at the moment the skier slows or stops his/her extension. This causes the ski to rebound, or spring back, propelling the skier out of the snow. The skier then turns and tips his/her skis before sinking into the snow and finishing the turn.

PERCEPTUAL SKILLS

Looking Ahead

In order to negotiate terrain changes or varying snow conditions smoothly, it is important to look ahead. Play follow-the-leader to encourage looking ahead. The leader must look down the hill in order to choose a smooth, interesting, or exciting path. He or she determines the size, shape, and speed of the turns. The follower stays in the leader's tracks by focusing on the path of the leader's skis, or by watching the leader's body movements.

Watch the leader's body movements

Adjusting Speed

The following exercise will help to develop your ability to increase or decrease the speed in which you descend a slope.

Find a skier who is moving at a consistent speed down the hill. Slow down to move farther away, or speed up to get closer to that skier. Be aware of the action that takes place in order to slow down. Experiment with a sharper turn that has a shorter radius, more turn completion, or skidded turns. In order to increase speed, choose a shallower turn arc, less turn completion, and minimize skidding.

Judging Distance

The ability to judge both speed and distance enables skiers to adapt to the demands of upcoming terrain.

To develop the skill of judging distances, pre-determine the number of turns it will take to ski from one point on the hill to another point that is farther down the hill. See if the number of turns that you selected actually brings you to the second point. Vary the designated number of turns to apply to small, medium, or large sized turns.

Mental Imagery

Imagine skiing precise and technically correct turns. It is important to imagine the feel, the sound and the appearance of excellent form, instead of merely observing other skiers as a spectator.

CHAPTER 5
DYNAMIC TURNS
Medium/Long Radius

Fast Through a Slow Turn

During the awards presentation at the Junior Olympic Championships, a young competitor was recognized for sportsmanship. He had told the race officials that he had missed a gate even though his name did not appear on the list of disqualifications. He had given up a top five Slalom result because he knew he did not deserve it. He said it would be unfair to the other racers. I applauded this young person, wondering more about him.

The following winter, Peter came to ski with us. It was as though he had always been on our team. He had a way of making everyone and everything seem important. Lost in an oversized jacket, quiet and thoughtful, Peter often represented his teammates. "I know a special place for a free-run," he would say just at the right moment when spirits were low. He brought our team closer and closer together, and as a result, everyone skied better.

Peter worked exceptionally hard on his technical skiing. He concentrated on carrying speed from one turn to the next by skiing precisely and accurately. Looking through my notebook now, I find notes I had written to Peter years ago: "...if you increase the angle at your hip, it will help you stay on the outside ski—the ski will continue in an arc and not slide away costing you valuable time in a race course."

By the time of the Junior Olympics, we had a chance of placing in the team competition for the first time ever. No one seemed more aware of this than the newest member of our team.

In the Giant Slalom, Peter went too straight right from the start. A less experienced skier would have thrown his skis sideways, getting back on line but losing considerable speed. Instead, Peter carried his speed, worked his turns cleanly and accurately, and gradually recovered his line.

At the finish, Peter was very quiet, thinking about his mistake. He had dropped out of the top five places. Then suddenly, a smile crept over his face and once again, his eyes began to dance. "I know my line was low," he said, "but did you see how fast I skied through those slow turns!" With unfailing spirit, he added, "I know a special place to ski," and he was off.

The most exciting moment of the event was when our whole team accepted the award for placing third in the team standings. Peter looked at me with a proud smile that clearly expressed, "I knew we could do it." What we had accomplished was far more important than our race results. We were winners in life. Peter was a perfect example.

CHAPTER 5
DYNAMIC TURNS – Medium/Long Radius

The skills that are acquired in Chapter 4, *Beginning Parallel Turns*, are refined in this chapter to develop *Dynamic Turns*. "Medium/long radius" refers to the size of the turn measured by the distance from the center of the turn to the arc (path of the skis). The medium and long radius turns described in this chapter are characteristic of Giant Slalom turns.

In dynamic medium/long radius turns, there is a more active commitment of the body into the turn with more deliberate edge usage and more accurate guiding of the skis throughout the turn. Turns are characterized by a strong flow of energy from one turn to the next. The intensity, duration and timing of the movements determine the size, shape and speed of the turn.

BALANCING EXERCISES

Lift Ski

Practice turning in both directions on one ski with the other ski raised in the air. Turning with the inside ski off the snow is described in Chapter 4, *Lift the Inside Ski*. Turning on the inside ski with the outside ski raised is more difficult. To accomplish this, begin on gentle terrain where your ski is fairly flat and, therefore, easier to turn on the snow surface. Plant your downhill pole firmly for support and pivot your inside (weighted) ski down the hill to start the turn. Lean to the inside of the turn and tip your inside ski on edge to control the arc of the turn. From this banked position, a deliberate pole plant down the hill will help you to move into the next turn. With practice, the pivoting action can be replaced with steering, a simultaneous turning *and* tipping of the ski onto the edge earlier in the turn.

One Ski

Practice medium radius turns on one ski with the other ski removed. Start on gentle terrain and progress to more demanding terrain. At some ski areas, permission to ski on one ski must be obtained from the ski area management.

Turning with one ski lifted

Turning with one ski removed

No Poles

Sometimes skiers drag their ski poles in the snow to compensate for an unbalanced stance. The lack of balance may be due to leaning uphill, turning with the upper body, or having too much weight on the tails of the skis. Skiing with one pole or without poles is a good test for balance.

To ski without poles, keep your upper body quiet and hold your arms in front of your body for balance. As you ski, focus on the balance point along the inside edge of your outside foot. This will enable you to regulate fore/aft balance and to stay balanced over your outside ski.

As your skills develop, return to this exercise regularly in order to evaluate your stance and to become aware of unnecessary upper body movements that compensate for weak lower body activity.

Skiing without poles

SKILL DEVELOPMENT

Balance Point

The balance point is the leverage point from which the ski is pressured and rotary movements are initiated. It is located at the back of the arch near the front of the heel. This body mass load point provides the most efficient location for rotary movement to take place.

In a static position, find the balance point on the sole of your foot. From this point, rock forward to feel your weight move toward the front of your foot (ski tip). Rock backward to feel your weight move toward the back of your foot (ski tail). Then move only as little as necessary, to feel your weight move toward the tip and then back toward the tail. Feel how very subtle body movements can change the distribution of weight. In general, only very small body movements are necessary to make fore/aft adjustments while skiing.

Rock forward

Rock backward

70

Fore/Aft Balance

In turns, use subtle movements to work from your balance point. Adjust your weight forward to start the turn, in the center through the turn, and slightly back for the turn completion. This action moves the concentration of pressure against the snow from the front to the back of the skis. It helps the skis travel forward through the arc of the turn without braking sideways.

Rock forward slightly

Hip Angulation

Angulation allows you to stay in balance on an edged ski by creating lateral angles in the body. Angulation can occur in the knees and hips (in conjunction with flexing these joints) and the spinal column. In a hip angulated position, the upper body stays relatively vertical, with shoulders level, while the lower body is at a slant to the snow.

To work on hip angulation, develop body angles by practicing either high speed, carved wedge turns on gentle terrain, or slower wedge turns on steeper terrain. Continue to focus on an angulated position when you return to a parallel stance.

Practice hip angulation in a wedge position

Wedge/Parallel

In this exercise the relationship between wedge and parallel turn positions becomes very clear. The leader turns in a narrow wedge position while the follower skis in a parallel position. The outside ski of the follower is placed in the track of the leader's outside ski. The follower (parallel skier) can observe the smooth arc of the turn, the action of the outside ski, and the body angles that are developed by the leader (wedge skier). The follower is forced to ski slowly, and therefore can concentrate on feeling the action of the outside ski and developing better body awareness.

Leader is in a wedge, follower is in a parallel position

Banking

Banking means leaning inward, inclining toward the inside of the turn with a relatively straight body position. This action usually weights the inside ski of the turn, and reduces the pressure on the outside ski. With less weight on the outside ski, it is difficult to keep it bent in an arc through the turn. Sideways slipping often results.

With angulation, more body weight is applied to the outside ski. Ski a series of banked turns followed by a series of angulated turns. Feel the difference between leaning inward with the entire body (banking), and leaning only with the lower body while keeping the upper body vertical (angulation).

Banking

Countered Position

In a traverse, a countered position means the downhill hip is slightly back in relation to the uphill hip. In a turn, the outside hip is slightly back in relation to the inside hip. A countered and hip angulated stance inhibits the ski tails from skidding through the finish of the turn. This position also directs the upper body toward the upcoming turn.

The *Advanced Traverse Exercises* described next are helpful for practicing a countered position while in a traverse. The *Javelin Turns* that follow encourage a countered position while in a turn.

Countered position

72

Advanced Traverse Exercises

The following advanced traverse exercises improve balance and edge control.

(a) Traverse across a steep slope. It is necessary to increase angulation and stand in a countered position in order not to "lose" the edge grip and slip sideways.

(b) On smooth terrain, step sideways to move your traverse line up the hill or down the hill.

(c) Lift the uphill ski. Flex and extend the downhill leg while traveling across the hill.

(d) Lift the downhill ski. Flex and extend the uphill leg while traveling across the hill.

(e) Traverse across medium sized bumps with your skis edged to maintain your line across the hill. Keep your upper body relatively still and absorb the terrain by bending and extending your legs. Let the bump bend your legs under your upper body as your skis climb up the bump. Then, rock forward and press your ski tips down the back, steep side of the bump to keep your skis on the snow.

Flex and extend the downhill leg

Extend and flex the uphill leg

Traverse across bumps

Javelin Turns

This exercise emphasizes a countered position with hip angulation. In a javelin, the skier balances on the outside ski of the turn with the inside ski lifted across the front of the outside ski. The placement of the inside ski makes it very difficult to rotate the outside hip through the turn.

Ski position in a javelin

Alternate, and repeat the following exercises to relate the hip and upper body position of javelin turns to turns with skis parallel:
  (a) six linked javelin turns, followed by
  (b) six turns lifting the inside ski parallel, followed by
  (c) six parallel turns placing the inside ski lightly on the snow

Also, try javelin turns without your ski poles. This requires a very accurate and balanced position.

Javelin turn without ski poles

Upper Body Direction

Finish turns in a slightly countered position (the uphill side of the body and uphill ski are slightly ahead) and aim your upper body toward the mid-way point of the next turn. In shallower turns, your upper body will aim more down the hill in comparison to larger changes of direction. Focus on completing each turn in position for the next turn.

Directing Extension

It is important that body extension movements carry the skier down the hill, and not vertically upward. Complete each turn with your upper body aimed toward the mid-way point of the upcoming arc. Extend in that direction.

Floaters

This exercise promotes early weight transfer and leg extension on the outside ski at the beginning of a turn. After completing a turn, transfer your weight to the uphill ski. Slowly extend as you traverse on this ski. Practice a smooth body extension, moving your body forward with the ski to "float" across the hill. Then tip this ski onto the inside edge, steering it into the next turn.

To develop *Floaters* into linked turns (without traverses), steer the tip of the uphill ski down the hill at the same time as you extend to direct your extension down the hill.

Floater

Flow

Focus on skiing from fall line to fall line to promote a continuous flow of movement through the transition phase between turns.

Building Pressure

At high speeds and on steep terrain, it is often necessary to build pressure through the end of the turn. Pressure keeps the outside ski bent in reverse camber, continuing the arc of the turn through completion. Pressure builds by resisting flexion of the outside leg or by extending against the outside ski.

This action can be felt by trying to push your outside foot through the snow, and extending your leg as you do so.

Building pressure on the outside ski

SKI POLE ACTION

Incorrect Pole Action

Being aware of incorrect pole and arm action will help
to avoid problems. Excessive arm movements can hinder balance. Following is a list of common faults:
  (a) improper timing of pole plants (too early or too
      late)
  (b) dropping the inside hand or lifting the outside hand
  (c) hands positioned too high or too low
  (d) planting out to the side
  (e) crossing arms in front of the body
  (f) forward movement of the shoulder
  (g) leaving the pole in the snow too long
  (h) relying on dragging the poles for balance
  (i) gripping the pole too tightly

Timing Exercise

The pole touch in medium/long radius turns should
coincide with the edge change during the beginning
phase of the new turn. Often skiers plant too early, at
the turn completion, disrupting the flow of movement
into the next turn. To encourage a later pole touch,
plant your pole twice: touch at the turn completion and
immediately afterward at the edge change. Then, elimi-
nate the first touch, and only touch your pole to change
edges.

TURN SHAPE

Carved Turns

Ski cleanly through the arc of each turn with precision
and accuracy. Start on gentle terrain, skiing slowly, and
then increase the speed of your turns. Progress to steeper terrain. Strive for smooth, continuous, carved turns
without losing the edge or using more edge than necessary.

Different Turn Shapes

Vary the intensity, duration, and timing of movements
to practice "C", "comma", and "J" shaped turns, as
described in *Technique*, Chapter 2.

Carved turn

76

Consistent Radius

On uneven terrain, practice skiing a consistent size turn. Look ahead to be prepared to absorb undulations in the terrain.

Varying Turns

On uneven terrain, vary the rhythm and radius of your turns to ski smoothly down the hill. On steeper pitches, complete your turns across the hill to control your speed. On flatter pitches, ski shallower arcs to carry speed.

TERRAIN/SNOW CONDITIONS

Gentle Terrain

Remember to return to gentle terrain to try new movements and to learn difficult maneuvers. In this way, you can improve your technique comfortably and then, when you feel ready, apply your skill to more challenging terrain.

It is also helpful to ski on gentle terrain in order to assess your progress. Slower speeds require more accuracy and precision, and difficulties are often magnified at slow speeds.

More Difficult Terrain

It is important to refine your skills and to perform consistently on "blue" terrain before you spend too much time on "black" terrain.

Most Difficult Terrain

Difficult terrain provides constant challenges for competent skiers. Miles of experience are necessary to adapt to demanding terrain and variable snow conditions.

Skiing demanding terrain

Adventure

Explore new terrain and different snow conditions (see *Hard Snow/Ice* and *Deep Snow*, Chapter 4). At all levels, the best racers are typically the best free-skiers.

Exploring new terrain

Bump Skiing

Bump skiing is helpful for developing balance, quickness and reactions (see *Bump Skiing*, Chapter 6). Strive for smooth flow of the upper body with only the legs moving up and down.

Skiing the bumps

78

PERCEPTUAL SKILLS

Judging Speed

On easy terrain, at a slow speed, ski as cleanly as possible through the arc of each turn, maximizing the speed for the situation. When the ski travels forward through the arc of the turn, it will carry more speed than if it skids sideways. In other words, ski fast through slow turns. Continue this theme for higher speed turns.

Free-ski/Course

Set short courses of four to six Slalom poles or *SAF T STIKS* at intervals down a long run. Ski the whole run moving smoothly from the course into free-skiing and back into the course. Look ahead to match the radius of the turns in the upcoming course.

This drill is excellent for developing perceptual skills since it requires skiers to rely on visual input in order to judge the speed, size, and shape of turns in relation to distance down the hill.

Listen to Ski Sounds

Listen to the sound that your skis make on a hard snow surface. Notice the louder sound when your skis skid sideways and the quieter sound when your skis travel forward through the arc of the turn. Work toward keeping your skis quiet on the snow.

Ski in and out of short courses

CHAPTER 6
DYNAMIC TURNS
Short Radius

The Shine and the Smile

"You won't believe how he skis." I was standing at the top of a steep Slalom course coaching twelve and thirteen-year-olds when I heard these words. That was my introduction to Chris.

I kneeled down to Chris' eye level and shook his big red mitten. He was small for a six-years-old and his goggles covered most of his face. Chris smiled shyly and then eyed the course and the much older skiers. "Have you ever run gates before?" I asked. He shook his head no in reply. "Would you like to ski this course?" His eyes became bigger as he nodded his goggles.

I watched in disbelief as this little skier became toy-like, playing in a land of giant poles. I had never imagined a young child could be capable of skiing so technically well. After a few runs, I asked Chris, "Are you ready to go faster?" Although his skiing was flawless, his line was excessively round and far from the gates. "Go a little straighter at the gates." This was a perfect example of the wrong choice of words. After every fourth or fifth gate, Chris would go straighter—actually straight down the hill, missing a couple of gates to reenter the course with more speed farther down the hill.

As Chris grew into his goggles, he continued to excel and lead his age group in race results.

After I moved away from my old program, I followed Chris' progress. Years later, I was surprised to hear that he had left skiing. At the time, Chris was ranked first for thirteen-year-olds in the Rocky Mountain Division. Finding my notebook, I looked for an old letter I had saved from Chris after I had moved away. He wrote, "I hope I never have to choose between skiing and tennis. I love to ski so much." That night, I called Chris. He said, "My coach hardly ever spoke to me and never in a positive way. It wasn't fun when I wasn't learning."

When I think of Chris, I am reminded of another little boy from a ski school class. When I asked him why he was taking a lesson, a big smile lit up his face, "to put a shine on my skiing, of course!" I realized the shine was important, but even more, the smile. Chris had lost both, and the ski world lost Chris.

DYNAMIC TURNS – Short Radius

Dynamic medium and long radius parallel turns provide the foundation for dynamic short radius turns. "Short Radius" refers to the size of the turn measured by the distance from the center of the turn to the arc (path of the skis). The short radius turns described in this chapter are characteristic of Slalom turns.

In short radius turns, weight is transferred onto the outside ski. This is followed by a strong turning of both skis as they are tipped on edge. The rhythm and pace of movements is quicker than in longer radius turns. The skier faces down the hill since there is not time for the upper body to follow the direction of the skis. The pole plant is used for blocking upper body rotation as well as for timing. In turns with a deliberate edge set, the pole plant and edge set occur at the same time. In gliding turns, the pole touch occurs a moment later, with the extension at the beginning of the next turn.

BALANCING EXERCISES

No Ski Poles

Skiing without poles encourages strong lower body skills as described in *No Poles* under *Skill Development* later in this chapter.

"Without" Bindings

While skiing, pretend that you do not have bindings on your skis. Instead, you must depend on standing in a centered and balanced body position in order not to fall off your skis. This exercise is especially helpful for skiers who sit back or hang forward against their boots.

Lift Ski

With one ski lifted off of the snow, smoothly link short radius turns on the other ski. Alternate sides.

Skiing without poles

One Ski

Smoothly link short radius turns on one ski with the
other ski removed. Turning on one ski is described in
Chapter 5, *Lift Ski*. For this exercise and the following
one ski exercises, permission to ski on one ski should be
obtained from ski area management.

Skiing on one ski

One Ski/One Pole

Ski on one ski with one ski pole. Start with the pole
that is on the same side of your body as your ski. The
pole plant will help to start the more difficult turn: the
turn on your inside ski. Alternate poles and skis.

Skiing on one ski with only one pole

One Ski/No Poles

Ski on one ski without poles. The hardest part about
this exercise is getting started. Since it is easier to turn
on your outside ski, make your first turn on that ski.
Lean to the inside of the next turn as you pivot or steer
your ski into that turn. It is helpful to establish a rhythm
in order to continue turning. Alternate sides.

Skiing on one ski without poles

SKILL DEVELOPMENT

Target Skiing

Target your upper body on an object down the hill such as a sign. Ski toward the object keeping your upper body quiet and constantly facing the target. Turning action should come from your legs only. Transfer weight from the outside ski of one turn to the outside ski of the next turn to help the timing and coordination of leg movements. Saying, "right foot, left foot," or, "right ski, left ski," in reference to weighting the appropriate outside foot/ski reinforces weight transfer and helps to establish a rhythm.

Using a sign as a target

Moving Target

Ski on gentle terrain behind a partner. The leader skis in a wedge straight down the hill. The follower uses the leader's back as an up-close target, constantly facing the target with the upper body.

Moving target

No Poles

Improve balance and the efficiency of your leg movements by skiing without ski poles.

As you ski, focus on the balance point along the inside edge of your outside foot in order to control the outside ski of the turn. Transfer weight from outside foot/ski to outside foot/ski. Aim your upper body down the hill. Maintain a quiet upper body with your arms held in front of your body for balance.

Arms held in front for balance

87

Arms Crossed

This exercise makes excessive upper body movements extremely apparent. Without your ski poles, cross your arms so that your hands touch your shoulders. Aim the cross of your arms down the hill. Make a deliberate weight transfer onto the outside ski. Then turn both skis as you tip them on edge. Some common problems are:
  (a) starting the turn with the upper body instead of with the legs
  (b) leaning the upper body into the turn
  (c) leaning and rotating into the turn
  (d) bending forward at the waist

Strive for a countered, angulated position to correct the errors.

Continue to focus on lower body action as you uncross your arms and ski without poles. Continue with this theme when you use your ski poles.

Aim the cross of your arms down the hill

Javelin with Arms Crossed

For added challenge and fun, practice javelin turns (see Javelin Turns, Chapter 5) with your arms crossed and aimed down the hill. The position of the inside ski makes it very difficult to rotate the outside hip through the turn.

Make sure to start each turn centered over your skis. As you transfer weight to the outside ski of each turn, stand on the balance point under your foot (back of the arch, near the front of the heel). If your weight does get back, it will be very difficult to keep your arms crossed and to face down the hill.

Javelin with arms crossed

Horizontal Pole

Without ski poles, hold a Slalom pole horizontally in front of your body. Ski short radius turns in the fall line keeping the pole level. When the pole tips toward the inside of the turn, the skier's upper body is leaning instead of staying upright. If the pole turns toward the inside of the turn, the skier's upper body is rotating instead of facing down the hill.

Keep the pole level

To improve, ski beside a competent partner, holding the Slalom pole horizontally in front of both of you. The partner and pole stabilizes the upper bodies of both skiers. This exercise encourages active lower body movement.

Stabilizing the upper body

88

Hop Turns

Hop turns develop strong lower body rotary movements of the legs underneath a non-turning upper body.

First, try hop turns without skis. Hop in place. Plant your right pole to turn to the right, plant your left pole to turn to the left. Use your pole plant to help you to spring upward. A solid pole plant supports and stabilizes the hopping action and helps to continue rhythm and movement. After you have added pole action, hop forward to move down the hill.

Next, try hop turns with one ski and then with the other ski. One-foot hop turns are easier to do than hop turns with both feet. There is less weight to lift and pivot.

With skis on, link rhythmic hop turns landing on and hopping off clean edges without skidding out. Maintain a balanced body position with the upper body facing down the hill.

Hop turns without skis

Hop turns on one ski

Hop turns with skis

Two Meter Drill

This drill develops strong lower body rotary skills, a quiet upper body, and an effective pole plant.

Set Slalom poles or *SAF T STIKS* in the fall line approximately two meters apart (the length of a 200 cm ski) on a moderate to steep slope. Link hop turns around the poles, landing on edged skis and hopping off edged skis, without skidding. Wait until your ski boots slide past each pole before you hop. Keep your upper body facing down the hill. Use a solid pole plant to support and stabilize the hopping action.

The *Two Meter Drill* can also be set in a moderate to steep traverse instead of along the fall line.

Link hop turns around poles

Hop Turn Entry

At the completion of a turn, plant your pole and hop, turning both skis down the hill. Land on both edges with more weight on the outside ski of the turn. Ski through the end of the turn. Practice a hop turn entry in turns to both directions, and then link turns.

Let this exercise evolve into smooth turns, without hopping. Replace the airborne rotary action with quick steering of the skis on the snow.

Hop to start a turn

Outside Ski Hop Turns

Hop turns from foot-to-foot strengthen your commitment to the outside ski. They are also beneficial for learning to get on and off your edges quickly. In addition, outside ski hop turns develop strong lower-body action beneath a quiet upper body.

First, try outside ski hop turns without skis. Stand with your feet turned slightly inward in a wedge position as you face down the hill. Hop off the inside edge of one foot and land on the inside edge of the other foot. Move your free leg next to the landing leg, but keep it off the snow. Continue hopping by alternating the push-off and landing feet. Press down on your right pole to help spring off your right foot, and press down on your left pole to help spring off your left foot.

Next practice the exercise with skis. Lay two Slalom poles in the snow forming a "V" on flat terrain. Use the Slalom poles as guides for ski placement. Hop within the "V" with your skis parallel to the poles. Hop from the inside edge of one foot/ski to the inside edge of the other. Land with your left ski next to the left pole, and on the next hop, land with your right ski next to your right pole. On each hop, the free leg is brought parallel to the landing ski.

Practice outside foot hops moving down the hill without skis, and then try the same pattern of movements with skis on.

Outside ski hop turns without skis

Outside ski hop turns

Use poles as guides for ski placement

91

Outside Ski Hop Turn Entry

At the completion of a turn, hop onto the inside edge of the new outside ski, directing it toward the fall line. Ski through the rest of the turn with the inside ski parallel to the outside ski. Link turns.

Evolve this exercise into a smooth turn entry with an early weight transfer and strong steering of the outside ski.

Hop onto the outside ski to start a turn

Direct the outside ski toward the fall line

Double Edge Set Drill

The *Double Edge Set Drill* requires accurate movements and precise timing. It is necessary to get on and off the edges quickly.

Set *SAF T STIKS* or stubbies (short Slalom poles) in the fall line approximately two and a half ski lengths apart on a moderate to steep slope. Turn under the first pole, and then turn again before reaching the second pole. Turn under the second pole, and so forth. In this way, you are making two turns (setting edges) for each pole. Alternate starting the course from both the right side and the left side of the first pole.

You can ease into this drill by practicing alongside the course and then moving closer to the poles until you are in the course. As you become more competent, set the poles closer, at two ski lengths apart.

Make two turns between consecutive poles

Garlands

Ski continuous short radius turns while traveling diagonally down the hill (review *Garland Turn Completion*, Chapter 4). Use the turn completion to work on the slicing action of the outside ski. Focus on the outside ski moving forward through the arc of the turn and not skidding out.

Rebound

Rebound can energetically propel a skier into the next turn.

In carved turns, the outside ski is bent into an arc ("reverse camber"). When the pressure that bends the ski is released, the ski springs back, or "rebounds." The rebound, or release of stored energy in the ski, can be directed to propel you into the next turn.

In order to create rebound, stay on your outside ski a moment longer than usual. This will tighten the radius of your turn and increase pressure on your ski. When you move into the next turn, your skis will flatten and the pressure will be released. The resultant bound of energy lightens your skis on the snow, or actually pops you into the air. At this time, turn and tip your skis to be in position to finish the turn as you touch down.

Formation Skiing

In formation skiing, two or more people ski together creating a pattern of turns. The three basic elements in formation skiing are synchronized turns, opposite synch, and lead-follow, described below. Participation in formation skiing promotes good rhythm and timing of movements as well as consistency and precision in performance. It is also an excellent activity for developing teamwork.

Synchronized Turns

In synchronized ("synchro") turns, two or more skiers turn in the same direction at the same time. The rhythm, radius, and speed of the turns are the same. Synchronized turns can be performed in horizontal, vertical or diagonal relationships.

Skiers turn in the same direction

Opposite Synchro

In opposite synchro turns, skiers perform the same turns while skiing in opposite directions. The rhythm, radius and speed of the turns are the same, just the direction changes.

Skiers turn in opposite directions

Lead-Follow

The follower skis in the leader's tracks. At first, focus on the leader's tracks in order to turn in the same place and not at the same time as the leader. With practice, you will be able to view the leader's movements but delay yours in order to start and complete each turn in his or her tracks.

SKI POLE ACTION

Verbal Cue

For rhythmic turns, a verbal cue such as "touch" or "plant" helps to time the action of the pole.

Pole Tip Forward

Short radius turns allow no time for excessive arm movements that can hinder balance. Use wrist movement to bring the pole tip forward instead of moving your whole arm. After touching the pole in the snow, roll your hand downward to pivot the pole off the snow.

Swing the pole tip forward

Surveyor's Tape

Use surveyor's tape to keep your hands in front of your body and to minimize arm movements. Surveyor's tape is safe to use for this exercise because it rips if large arm movements become necessary for balance. It can be found at most hardware stores.

Hold your hands apart, a few inches wider than your body. Measure a piece of surveyor's tape the same width plus a few inches to wrap around your hands. First without poles, ski a series of short radius turns aiming the tape down the hill. Then wrap the ends of the tape around the grips of your poles. The tape will restrict your hands from moving unnecessarily as you plant your poles.

Keep hands in front

Pole plant while keeping hands in front

Synchronized Skiing

With synchronized turns, a less skilled skier can improve by copying the rhythm and timing of a partner's pole plants when he or she skis beside or behind the partner. The moment of pole touch can also be used to signal the timing of synchronization.

Pole plant at the same time

Double Pole Plant

To double pole plant, swing and touch the outside pole at the same time as you swing and touch the inside pole of the turn. This drill helps skiers to:
  (a) get up and forward in order to be centered coming into a new turn
  (b) position both hands up and forward
  (c) maintain level shoulders
  (d) stabilize turning movements of the shoulders

Error Recognition and Correction

Work with a partner to evaluate each other's pole plants. Look for symmetry in the right and left pole plants. Efficient and effective pole usage means eliminating any unnecessary hand, arm, and upper body movements.

Double pole plant

TURN SHAPE

Vary Turns

Short radius turns can be different in shape, size, and speed. Vary your turns as you ski. Envision open and tight slalom turns, rhythm changes, and flush, hairpin, and delay gate combinations (refer to *Race Skills for Alpine Skiing*).

Smooth Transitions

Vary the size of your turns to include short, medium and long radius turns during one run.

Before changing to short radius turns, stay longer on the outside ski of the last medium or long radius turn to tighten the radius and assist in the transition. Complete your last medium or long turn across the hill, or even slightly up the hill in order to slow your speed. Face your upper body down the hill in preparation for short radius turns.

In the transition from short to medium or long radius turns, finish the last short turn closer to the fall line to gain speed. Aim your upper body toward the mid-way point of the arc for the longer radius turn.

Rhythm Changes

Ski a series of turns that are consistent in rhythm, and then change the rhythm for the next series of turns. For example, alternate five medium radius turns with ten short radius turns. By choosing an odd number of turns in one radius, and an even number of turns in the other radius, transitions from one radius to the other will occur in both directions.

Lead-Follow

As the leader, vary the radius of your turns. As the follower, try to stay in the leader's tracks.

TERRAIN/SNOW CONDITIONS

Adapt to Terrain

Try to maintain rhythmic, short radius turns for a very long run, regardless of the terrain. This task encourages you to perform consistently, control your speed, and adapt to the demands presented by varying terrain.

Versatility

To develop versatility, practice turns in all kinds of terrain including steeps, transitions, side hills and bumps, and in all kinds of snow conditions including ice, powder, and crud (see *Terrain/Snow Conditions*, Chapter 4).

Side Hill Terrain

On a side hill, the slope falls away from the skier's direction of travel. A good weight transfer to the outside ski is very important for side hill, fall-away turns. Practice garland turns in preparation for side hill terrain (see *Garland Turn Entry* and *Garland turn Completion*, Chapter 4).

Steep Terrain

Skiers often find their weight back when they start down steep terrain. From this position, it is difficult to turn and to control speed. A short section of outside-ski hop turns can help you to:
(a) find a stance that is perpendicular to the slope of the hill.
(b) create the strong rotary action that is necessary to turn your skis across the hill and control your speed.
(c) commit to the outside ski of the turn in order not to lean up the hill. Leaning would decrease the edge angle and therefore, the ability to grip on a steep slope.

Deep Snow

The following tactical considerations are helpful for making the transition from hard snow to deep snow:
(a) ski rhythmic turns in, or close to the fall line
(b) start with shallow arcs
(c) ski steeper terrain to maintain speed
(d) as speed increases, round-out the turns

Also consider the following technical aspects:
(a) weight is distributed equally on both skis
(b) stance is narrow, yet legs remain independent of each other
(c) active flexion and extention movements
(d) upper body faces down the hill
(e) both skis are turned at the same time with rotary action of the legs

Side hill, fall-away turn

Skiing steep terrain

Weight is distributed equally on both skis

Crud Snow

Since snow conditions are so changeable, concentrate on the balance point under your foot when you ski crud snow. Fore/aft adjustments are often necessary to ski through snow of different depths and densities smoothly.

Crud snow

Bump Skiing

Skiing in the bumps promotes balance and the ability to adapt quickly to abrupt terrain changes. Elements to focus on include:
  (a) keeping your hands forward
  (b) using a deliberate pole plant
  (c) looking ahead to choose a line
  (d) committing your upper body down the hill
  (e) pressing your ski tips down the back, steep side of bumps (or lifting the tails of your skis to accomplish the same thing)
  (f) maintaining contact of the skis on the snow
  (g) staying in the fall line
  (h) skiing long distances

Keep your hands forward

Line in the Bumps

There are many different approaches a skier can take in order to choose a path, or "line" in the bumps. Some of the variables involved are:
  (a) the steepness of the hill
  (b) the speed of descent
  (c) the distance between bumps
  (d) the shape of the bumps (round, sharp, drop-off)
  (e) the depth of the troughs between bumps

As the pitch of the hill increases, speed control becomes more of a factor. Speed is decreased by turning the skis farther across the hill, increasing the edge angle, and/or minimizing the time in the fall line. Skiers can choose to ski closer to the fall line, or to round-out their turns in order to ski faster or slower respectively. Skiers can carry greater speed when bumps are farther apart. With bumps that are closer together, the skier's turns become tighter. Slower speeds result.

Look ahead to choose a line

Line in the Bumps (continued)

Sharp bumps or drop-offs require more aggressive absorption movements of the legs in comparison to smooth, round-shaped bumps. Since your weight can get thrown forward or backward with abrupt terrain changes, constantly seek the balance point on your foot. This is also essential for staying in balance when your skis accelerate quickly in a trough. The deeper the troughs become, the less opportunity you have to determine where and when you want to turn.

The unpredictable nature of bumps requires a spontaneous combination of the following approaches, as well as tremendous quickness and balance. Look ahead to choose the smoothest line, and be ready to change your tactics as the terrain demands. Different lines in the bumps are:
   (a) turning sharply on the tops of bumps
   (b) staying in the troughs
   (c) turning on the banked side of bumps
   (d) hitting the tops of bumps

Turning sharply on the top of bumps is a common way to begin bump skiing (see *Small Bumps*, Chapter 4) A relatively flat area on the uphill side, or top of each bump, provides room to turn and edge skis sharply. Speed is decreased in this way. Turning sharply on the bump is also used by highly-skilled bump skiers in order to slow their speed quickly .

Troughs are the carved-out channels between bumps. They often form a zig-zag pattern down the hill. As you cross the rise that separates one trough from the next, flex your legs to absorb the pressure that builds as your skis climb the rise. Then extend your legs into the trough, pressing your ski tips down to contact the snow. As your skis descend into the trough, they accelerate quickly and may get slightly ahead of your upper body. The deceleration of your skis at the transition between turns allows your upper body to re-center over your feet.

A smooth, round line can be skied by turning on the banked sides of bumps. Rather than being in the trough, the skier is above it, on the side of the adjacent bump. Ski across the top of the trough instead of turning into it. Then turn on the side of the adjacent bump. Tighten the turn radius to cut through the end of the turn in order to control speed and to be in position to start the next turn.

In comparison, a straighter line can be skied by hitting the tops of the bumps and turning in the air. The skier lands on the bump with skis that are already redirected and edged to momentarily slow speed. For this approach, it is important that the skier be extended in flight in order to be in position to flex and absorb the impact of landing.

Different Paths

Start from different locations at the top of a bump run to explore different paths through the bumps.

Adjust Direction

Pre-determine a finish zone on the right or left side, or in the center at the bottom of the bump run. As you ski, work your way toward the particular finish zone that you have chosen. This challenge requires looking ahead and determining moves instead of reacting to terrain.

PERCEPTUAL SKILLS

Mind Set

In your mind, visualize skiing a run that you know well. Decide what turns to make in order to control or maintain speed when the pitch of the slope changes.

Imagine setting a course to include rhythm changes which correspond to changes in terrain. Where on the hill should rounder turns be set to control speed? Where should gates be set closer to the fall line to let skis run? How should gates be set to bring the course across the hill?

Racer Set

Have each racer set and then run their own course. This is important for being able to associate gate placement across the hill in relation to distance down the hill. The racer will have to take speed into account while judging distances. See *Race Skills for Alpine Skiing*, published by the Turning Point Ski Foundation for more information on course setting and racing.

Setting a course

102

CHAPTER 7
STEP TURNS

The Day the Results Blew Away

As I turned the pages of my old notebook, I noticed a newspaper article: "Jon Nolting, whose best previous finish was 16th, skied to a phenomenal third place in the J3 Giant Slalom event. He had turned in a fast time for the first run on the long, steep, windblown course, and ran nearly last in the starting order for the second run. He didn't know how he had finished until the awards ceremony, since his unofficial results blew off the scoreboard."

Jon had worked his way up through our program starting with the Training Squad. From the beginning, Jon was always the first one on the mountain and he didn't come in until after the lifts had closed—sometimes, not even then. He always carried food in his pocket and disappeared up the mountain when the others went in for lunch. He didn't ski in the usual places. Jon could be found skiing the steepest terrain, the most difficult bumps and the worst snow conditions around. When he couldn't be found, he would be blazing trails through the trees.

Jon built his own ski area, "Nolting Basin," in his backyard. It was complete with trail map and snow depth readings. Every weekday he would hike the hill after school and ski until dark.

Jon became known for his eagerness to learn, dedication to practice, and most of all, his knowledge of the best places to ski on the mountain. It was no wonder Jon performed so well on the demanding race course on that windy day.

The newspaper article ended: "At the awards ceremony, Jon earned the loudest and longest applause of any competitor as his name was announced."

Step turns are dynamic parallel turns that are initiated with a parallel step, converging step or diverging step. Step turns allow you to change your path
of descent quickly and efficiently. This is often necessary in a sport which has so many variables. It is
helpful to have different turn options in order to
meet the demands of changeable terrain, uneven sur-
faces, and inconsistent snow conditions.

Stepping at the beginning of a turn can increase or
decrease the size of a turn and the speed of the skier.
Stepping can be used to avoid obstacles and to move
to preferable terrain.

In this chapter, *Step Turns* are divided into three
parts:
  A. Parallel Step Turns
  B. Converging Step Turns
  C. Diverging Step Turns

A. PARALLEL STEP TURNS

A parallel step is used to gain a slightly higher line.
This may be necessary to change your line in bumps or
race courses. A parallel step can also be used to change
the position of the skis in relation to the body. With a
step, the outside ski of the new turn is moved under the
body and up the hill. This positions the body to the
inside of the line the skis will travel through the arc of
the new dynamic turn. It is a very efficient way to
acquire an edge early in the turn.

Parallel steps are suitable for flat and steep terrain. A
parallel step is less effective in deep snow conditions,
where it is better to have weight distributed on both
skis.

To start a parallel step turn, step the uphill ski laterally
(sideways) up the hill. Place the stepped ski parallel to
the downhill ski. Transfer your weight to the stepped
ski and steer it into a turn. Move the inside ski closer to
the outside ski as you complete the dynamic parallel
turn. The pole swing occurs with or after the step, and
continues with the leg extension on the new outside ski,

Parallel step turn

helping to direct the body into the turn. The pole touch occurs when the outside ski tips onto the inside edge. Tipping of the ski refers to the movement from the uphill edge to flat and then to the downhill edge.

A parallel step is also known as an "inside/outside" or "inside/flat" move, referring to the edge usage.

BALANCING EXERCISES

Side Step Over Pole

Stand beside a ski pole or a Slalom pole laid on the snow. Step the ski that is closest to the pole over the pole and stand on it momentarily before bringing it back to its original place. Cross this ski back and forth over the pole to practice a parallel step, weight transfer, and balance on one ski.

Step one ski back and forth

Step Drills

Lay three or more Slalom poles on the snow in the fall line or in a traverse on nearly flat terrain. Step one ski over the first pole and then the other ski. Step far enough sideways to allow room for the second ski. Cross back and forth over the poles in this manner.

Lay several Slalom poles along a traverse line with each succeeding pole set about twelve inches up the hill. Starting in a traverse on the downhill side of the first pole, step uphill over the pole with both skis to a traverse line below the second pole. Step over that pole and repeat for each succeeding pole.

Cross over the pole

SKILL DEVELOPMENT

Parallel Step

As you traverse across the hill, step your uphill ski up the hill and momentarily place it *parallel* to the position of the downhill ski. Then return the uphill ski to its original position. Repeatedly step in this manner. Practice this exercise while crossing the hill in both directions.

Step up the hill

Parallel Step Garland

Parallel Step Garlands can be used for the repetitive practice of steering the skis down the hill after a parallel step occurs (see *Garland Turn Entry*, Chapter 4). Start in a traverse. Step up the hill, weight the uphill ski, and steer both skis slightly down the hill. Before reaching the fall line, transfer weight to your original downhill ski. Finish in a turn continuing in the direction of your initial traverse. Repeatedly step and turn in this manner while crossing the hill in both directions.

Parallel step garland

Parallel Step Garland, Turn

Cross a hill doing the *Parallel Step Garland* exercise. After the last garland, complete a turn in order to resume *Parallel Step Garlands* while traveling in the other direction.

Traverse, Step and Turn

Starting in a traverse, perform a parallel step up the hill. The stepped ski becomes the outside ski of a turn as you weight this ski and steer both skis through the entire turn. Link traverses, parallel steps and turns.

Step and Turn

Decrease the length of the traverse between turns until the completion of one turn leads into the parallel step turn entry of the next turn.

Parallel step garlands and turn

Review

Review and practice *Upper Body Direction*, *Directing Extension* and *Floaters*, Chapter 5. The movement patterns described in these exercises are applicable to parallel step turns. *Floaters* use a weight transfer without a step, but are otherwise similar to *Parallel Step Turns*.

Vary Radius

Practice a parallel step in short, medium and long radius turns to become proficient in this maneuver.

B. CONVERGING STEP TURNS

In converging step turns, the outside ski is directed toward the fall line early in the turn, cutting off the top of the turn. A converging step is used to move quickly into the fall line and onto the inside edge of the new outside ski. Converging step turns can be used on all terrain. They are effective on very steep terrain where it is necessary to minimize the time spent turning into the fall line in order to get the skis quickly across the hill for the purpose of controlling speed. A converging step turn is very effective for getting started in deep snow and on steep terrain.

To start a converging step turn, stem the uphill ski to create a converging relationship with ski tips together and tails apart. Move from the inside edge of your downhill ski (of the previous turn) to the inside edge of your new uphill ski (new outside ski). The converging action points your ski down the hill. Step onto an edged ski. The pole swing coincides with the stemming action and the pole touches as the inside edge engages. Bring the inside ski parallel and complete the turn as a dynamic parallel turn.

A converging step is also known as an "inside/inside" move or "stem step", referring to the edge usage.

Converging step turn

BALANCING EXERCISES

Converging Steps in a Circle

On flat terrain, step your ski tails around in a circle, pivoting around the tips of your skis. Repeat, stepping in the other direction.

Step around the tips of your skis

Wagon Wheel

On flat terrain, lay eight Slalom poles on the snow with one end of all of the poles touching to form the spokes of a wagon wheel. Step over each pole as described in *Converging Steps*, facing the center of the wheel. For small children, add poles (additional spokes) so that the converging step is in proportion to their size.

Step over each pole

Step Drill

Set the *Step Drill* close to the fall line, on nearly flat terrain. Lay poles at angles on the snow as pictured Step to cross over each pole as you reach the junction between poles. The outside ski must be stemmed in order to place it parallel to the pole.

SKILL DEVELOPMENT

Converging Step

As you traverse across the hill, stem your uphill ski, touching it *lightly* on the snow. After each stem, return the uphill ski to its original position. Repeatedly step in this manner. Practice this exercise while crossing the hill in both directions.

Stem your uphill ski

Converging Step Garland

Converging Step Garlands can be used for the repetitive practice of starting into a turn after the converging step occurs (see *Garland Turn Entry*, Chapter 4). Start in a traverse. Stem the uphill ski up the hill, weight both skis, and steer them slightly down the hill. Before reaching the fall line, transfer weight to your original downhill ski. Finish in a turn in order to continue in the direction of your initial traverse. Repeatedly stem and turn in this manner while crossing the hill in both directions.

Converging step garland

113

Traverse, Stem and Turn

Starting in a traverse, perform a converging step up the hill. The stepped ski becomes the outside ski of a turn as you weight this ski and steer both skis through the entire turn. Link traverses, converging steps and turns.

Stem and Turn

Decrease the length of the traverse between turns until the completion of one turn leads into the stem entry of the next turn, leaving out the traverse.

Fall Line Converging Turns

To develop quick converging steps in the fall line, practice *Outside Ski Hop Turns*, Chapter 6. Follow this exercise with short radius turns, starting each turn by hopping onto the inside edge of the newly stemmed outside ski. Let this exercise evolve into quick converging step turns by stepping instead of hopping onto the outside ski.

C. DIVERGING STEP TURNS

A diverging step is used to gain a higher line, particularly in a race course. The diverging step is also effective for removing pressure from the outside ski. When weight is transferred onto the flatter inside ski, there is less resistance, allowing the ski to glide faster. Diverging step turns are more appropriate on moderate terrain where turn completion on the outside ski is not essential for speed control.

Before the completion of a dynamic parallel turn, pivot the inside ski across the hill. This creates a diverging relationship with ski tails together and tips apart. Step onto the uphill edge of this inside ski. The pole swing occurs with or after the step, and continues with the leg extension on the new outside ski, helping to direct the body into the turn. The pole touch occurs when the new outside ski tips onto the inside edge. Bring the inside ski parallel and complete the turn as a dynamic parallel turn.

The diverging step is also known as an "inside/outside"

Diverging step turn

114

move, referring to the edge usage.

A common variation of the diverging step turn incorporates the divergent relationship without the stepping action. In this turn, transfer weight to the inside ski and continue the steering action as this ski becomes the outside ski of the next turn. Weight is transferred without a stepping action.

The diverging step is also known as an "inside/outside" move, referring to the edge usage.

BALANCING EXERCISES

Diverging Steps in a Circle

On flat terrain, step your ski tips around in a circle, pivoting around the tails of your skis. Repeat, stepping in the other direction.

Step around the tails of your skis

Wagon Wheel

Lay eight Slalom poles on the snow with one end of all of the poles touching to form the spokes of a wagon wheel. Step over each pole as described in *Diverging Steps*, but now face the outside of the wheel. For small children, add poles so that the diverging step is in proportion to their size.

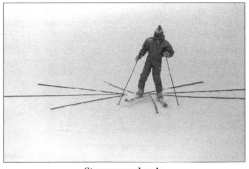

Step over each pole

115

SKILL DEVELOPMENT

Fall Line Skate

Skate down the fall line of a gentle hill. Push off with one ski and move your upper body over the other ski as you glide on its outside edge. Bring your feet together before pushing off onto the other ski (see *Skating on Flat Terrain*, Chapter 4).

Skate down the fall line

Skate Race

You can practice diverging steps with a partner in a race across flat terrain. This skating exercise helps develop a deliberate weight transfer off an edged ski.

Fall Line Skate and Turn

After gliding onto the outside edge as described in the *Fall Line Skate* exercise, tip your ski onto the inside edge and steer it into a shallow turn. Finish with your skis parallel, ready to skate into the next turn.

Skate race

Steep Traverse, Skate and Turn

Start from a steep traverse. Skate onto the outside edge of your uphill ski and then steer it into the turn. Practice this turn in both directions.

Skate and Turn

Link turns so that the completion of one turn leads into the skate entry of the next turn.

Steer the Inside Foot

Without skis, draw arcs in the snow with the inside foot of the turn. Concentrate on the steering action of the foot. Try to capture this same feeling and action while skiing.

Early Weight Transfer

Actively steer the inside ski and transfer your weight to this ski before the turn is completed.

Extension

Extend on the gliding, inside ski, moving in the direction of the upcoming turn. The extension flattens the ski, making it easier to steer into the turn.

GLOSSARY

Aerodynamic: the position a skier assumes in order to cut through the air with the least amount of air resistance.

Angulation: creating lateral angles in the body that enhance balance. Angulation can occur in the knees and hips (in combination with flexing of these joints) and the spinal column.

Arc: the curved path of the ski in the snow.

Balancing point: a point on the foot that is located near the back of the arch, in front of the heel. Subtle fore and aft movements originating from this point allow skiers to adjust weight forward to start the turn, centered through the turn, and slightly back for the completion of the turn.

Balanced stance: the skier's center of mass (weight) lies in a vertical plane that is perpendicular to the skis and passes through the balancing point.

Banking: leaning inward (inclining toward the inside of the turn) with a relatively straight body position.

Carving: weighting and angulating the ski so that it bends into a circular arc, whereby the edge of the ski moves along a corresponding circular arc to form a sharp curved track in the snow. In pure carving, every point along the length of the ski follows the same path along the arc of the turn and there is no skidding.

Chatter: the edge of the ski catches in the snow and bounces repeatedly to a lower path. Chatter can occur when the edge of the ski is at too steep of an angle.

Countered position: the outside hip is slightly back in relation to the inside hip in a traverse or turn. Countering movements generally occur with angulation of the hip and spine.

Cross-over transition: the skier's body crosses over the skis during the transition between turns.

Cross-under transition: the skier's legs quickly move laterally under the body during the transition between turns.

Crud snow: snow that is inconsistent in depth and density.

Curvilinear: a line or path that curves.

Directed free skiing: focus of attention on specific technical or tactical elements while skiing.

Dynamic: refers to the rapid adjustments of body position that the skier makes to stay in balance.

Edging: tipping of the ski onto one of its edges.

Edge angle: the amount a ski is tipped on edge. The edge angle is measured relative to a horizontal surface.

Fall line: through any point on the hill, the fall line is the direction where the hill has the steepest slope. A snowball will roll in that direction.

Garland: incomplete turn that results in diagonal travel down a hill. Garland turns provide an effective exercise for practicing the entry or completion phase of a turn repeatedly.

Gliding: implies carved turns in which skiers maximize speed by using the least amount of edge angle necessary to maintain their line through the gates.

Hip angulation: an angle at the hip between the upper body and lower body. The upper body stays relatively vertical, with shoulders level, while the lower body is at a slant to the snow. This is a strong position because the skeletal alignment from the foot to the hip provides support.

Inside ski: considering that a turn is part of a circle, the inside ski is closer to the center of the circle.

Javelin: an exercise in which the skier balances on the outside ski of the turn while the inside ski is lifted across the front of the outside ski. The placement of the inside ski encourages a countered position and makes it very difficult to rotate the outside hip through the turn.

Line: the skier's path down a bump run of a race course.

Linked turns: the completion of one turn leads directly into the start of the next turn.

Open stance: the skis are apart in a position that is comfortable and stable.

Outside ski: considering that a turn is part of a circle, the outside ski is farther from the center of the circle.

Over-edging: using more edge than is necessary for a given situation.

Pivoting: twisting of a flat ski by rotating the foot about an axis perpendicular to the surface of the snow. The skier's direction of travel does not changed.

Pressure control: adjustments a skier makes to control the location of the center of force acting on the skis. Weight transfer from ski to ski, fore/aft movements, and flexing/extending actions effect the amount and location of pressure on a ski.

Radius: distance from the center of a circle to the edge of the circle. Tight turns in which the center of the turn is close to the track of the ski are referred to as short radius turns. When the distance between the turn center and ski track is great, turns are considered to be long radius turns. In racing, Slalom turns are generally classified as short radius turns. Giant Slalom turns are medium radius, and Super-G and Downhill turns are long radius turns.

Railed ski: an edged ski that tracks straight ahead. Typically, a skier's intention is to turn when railing occurs.

Rebound: the springing back, or recoiling of a ski that has been bent in reverse camber.

Reverse Camber: camber is the bend in a ski that is apparent when the bases of two skis are placed together. Camber distributes the weight of a skier along the running surface of a ski. Reverse camber occurs when the camber is pressed flat and the ski bows in the other direction. This happens when a ski is bent in an arc during a turn.

Rhythmic turns: a series of turns of the same radius and speed.

Rotary action: the action of turning or twisting the

body along its vertical axis.

Rotary leg movements: the turning or twisting movement of the legs beneath a stable upper body.

Safety stop: pivoting of the skis into a sideslip and increasing edging to come to a stop.

Side-cut: the difference in width of a ski at its tip, tail and middle. Skis are wider at the tip and tail in comparison to the middle of the ski. In general, the more side-cut a ski has, the sharper it will turn.

Side hill: the slope falls away from the skier's direction of travel.

Skidding: a combination of sliding, slipping and pivoting resulting in a turn.

Slipping: sideways travel of a flat ski.

Sliding: forward travel of a flat ski.

Steering: an additional torque that is applied to change the path of the ski from the path of pure carving. The torque causes a pivoting action, such that steering always adds a skidding motion to the ski. Steering is applied to decrease the radius of an otherwise pure carved turn.

Straight run: when a skier slides straight down a slope while standing in a balanced position with weight distributed equally on both skis.

Stubby poles: flex poles, about two feet tall, that are used in drill courses. "Stubbies" allow skiers to ski close to a pole without having to clear the pole away with the upper body.

Synchronize: two or more skiers start and finish turns at the same time. Skiers can be in a horizontal, vertical or diagonal formation, or no fixed formation.

Tactics: the racer's line through the course. The term, *tactics*, can also apply to the racer's plan or strategy for skiing the course.

Technique: how the formal elements of skiing are performed. Technique is usually evaluated by comparison with optimum body positions and ski positions for every type of maneuver encountered in free-skiing or racing. Optimum technique is a constantly evolving quality, subject to the current judgment of coaches, racers and skiing authorities.

Traverse: gliding across a hill in a parallel ski relationship on uphill edges.

Trough: carved out channels between bumps.

Tuck: a compact, aerodynamic body position in which the back of the skier is essentially parallel to the surface of the skis.

Under-edging: using less edge than is necessary for a given situation.

DOWNHILL TUCK

It is very common to see a young skier "drop into a tuck" to ski across flat terrain. For this reason, it is necessary to learn to tuck safely, and to know when and where it is appropriate.

Safety

In order to ski safely in a tuck position, you must be familiar with the terrain and always look ahead. Be prepared to come out of your tuck and slow your speed at any time in order to avoid potentially dangerous situations. Ski a safe distance from people, trees, edges of trails, and obstacles. It is essential to wear a helmet that fits properly (see *Helmets*, Appendix II).

Being in a tuck does not necessarily mean skiing at a high speed. Fast skiing should be done in controlled training areas only. While free skiing, a tuck position can help skiers cross flat terrain where speeds are relatively slow.

Low Tuck Position

A tuck is a compact, aerodynamic body position. Characteristics of a low tuck position include:
  (a) Center your weight over both feet and skis.
  (b) Place your feet and knees an equal distance apart. The optimum distance is one that allows you to maintain flat skis on the snow. It is different for each skier, depending upon individual anatomy and ski boot cant.
  (c) Slightly round your back so that it is essentially parallel to the surface of your skis. Your upper leg (thigh) is nearly parallel to the ski, too, but your thigh and chest should not be in contact.
  (d) Hold your arms in front of your body with your elbows positioned over the outer part of your knees.
  (e) Hold your hands close together, with your arms either extended with a slight bend at the elbows, or bent more to bring your hands up and near your face.
  (f) Lift your head sufficiently to look ahead, down the hill.

Learning the tuck position

Low tuck position

High Tuck Position

For a high tuck, start in a low tuck and extend your legs. From this taller position, you have the ability to bend and extend your legs in order to absorb abrupt changes in terrain. You can open your arms in a forward direction for balance, or you can keep your hands together, with your poles tucked under your arms.

More information concerning downhill tucks can be found in the book, *Race Skills for Alpine Skiing*, published by the Turning Point Ski Foundation.

EQUIPMENT

For young skiers, the right equipment and the right fit is essential.* Equipment alone cannot make a champion, but it can prevent one from developing. Children can and should learn sound technique from the outset, and the appropriate equipment is a necessary prerequisite for good technical skiing.

Most skiers have experienced, at one time or another, the discomfort and frustration of poorly fitting ski boots, or unsuitable or badly tuned skis. It is important for coaches, instructors and parents to recognize the equipment needs of their young skiers. The wrong equipment can encourage the development of bad habits, which are then difficult to break—even on the right equipment. Guidelines for selecting equipment and suiting it to the size and ability of a skier follow.

Boots

Ski boots should permit a balanced, natural stance. A young skier does not have the strength to bend a stiff boot. A boot should be soft (flex forward without great force) so that a child can flex it comfortably. A soft boot that will "give" allows a child to use subtle movements to control his or her skis. The sense of balance learned in a soft boot will help a child to develop a light touch on the skis and a "feel" for the snow. Since a child's feet can grow to be quite big at a young age, he or she may need a large boot size. Regardless of size, the boot should flex without great resistance. If a skier's boots are too stiff, ski shop personnel may be able to modify them so that they can be flexed more easily.

Typically, tall ski boots are relatively stiff, and therefore, a short, softer boot is preferred. The boot opening should not be too wide for the skier's lower leg. The cuff of the boot should fit snugly around the leg in order to minimize leg movement relative to the boot.

Choose a four buckle, front-entry boot rather than a rear-entry boot. Four buckle boots can give a more personal fit and place a skier in a better balanced position. Rear-

* Some of the material in this section appeared in "Go for Fit, Flex When Choosing Kid's Gear," by Ellen Post Foster and Emily Katz Anhalt, *The Professional Skier,* Fall 1994.

entry boots may not provide enough support when a skier's weight moves against the back of the boot. When flexed, they usually do not "give" but spring back instead. This can cause the skier's weight to move back toward his or her heels. Then, too, with a looser fit, the foot tends to slide forward in the boot and the skier's weight shifts back.

To determine if a child's boots fit properly, follow these steps:

(a) Remove the liner from the shell.
(b) Have the child step into the shell, and while standing, slide his or her foot forward so that the toes just touch the end of the shell. There should be a 1/2–3/4 inch gap between the heel and the back of the shell to allow for the liner. Place your fingers in the shell to estimate the width of the gap.
(c) Have the child put on the liner. He or she should wear one pair of warm socks. There should be enough room so that the toes do not press into the end of the liner.
(d) With the liner in the shell, adjust the buckles so that the boots fit snugly. Have the child flex forward as you buckle each boot in order to push the heel into the back of the liner.
(e) Ask the child if his or her feet hurt. Try to identify the exact location of any sore spots. Then take off the boots and socks and look for any red marks which may indicate pressure points. Ski shop personnel can often correct any problems.

Have the child walk around in the boots and go up and down stairs, holding the railing or your hand. The child should be able to walk reasonably well. If he or she is very clumsy and unbalanced, the boots may be too stiff, too tall, too large, or a combination of these. In a boot that is too large, the foot can move excessively and be unstable while skiing. A boot that is too small can cause pain, numbness and cold feet.

To determine if a child can flex a boot sufficiently, ask the child to move down and up from a tall stance by bending the ankle. This action can be practiced first without boots to attain the correct body position. Watch to see if the child sits back or bends forward in an effort to flex the boot. Either of these movements indicate that the boot is too stiff. Another test is to have the child jump since jumping is very difficult when boots are too stiff.

126

To minimize wear from walking, it is helpful to use boot sole protectors, plastic guards that attach to the bottom of ski boots.

Skis

Children's skis must flex easily if they are to perform well. A skier's body weight presses (bends) an edged ski into an arc to make a turn. If skis are too stiff, they will not stay in an arc; sideways skidding will occur.

Selection of the best length and model of skis will depend on a child's size and ability level. A longer ski is more stable at high speed while a shorter ski is more manageable and easier to turn. Follow these general guidelines to check for appropriate ski length.
  (a) Beginning skiers, or very young children: shoulder height skis are easy to maneuver.
  (b) Intermediate skiers: skis that reach somewhere between the nose and the top of the head. Skiers at this level can handle a little longer ski that is still easy to maneuver.
  (c) Advanced skiers: skis that are as tall as their height and up to a height of the width of their hand above their head. This length allows skiers to be stable at higher speeds.
  (d) Technically strong or heavier racers who ski three or more days per week: longer skis which range from a height of their hand's width above the head up to the height of the wrist when their arm is extended. Skiers at this level should have the technical skills that are necessary to ski on longer skis.

Measuring ski length

Judgment plays a significant role in ski selection. A very tall, thin child, for example, may be better off with a ski measured at the lower end of the size range, whereas a sturdier child may do well with a longer length. Junior skis generally measure as tall as size 182cm. Adult skis usually start at 180cm, but they are considerably stiffer than junior skis. Select a junior ski whenever possible.

Equipment manufacturers offer a variety of skis and recommend different models to meet different needs. Flex, side-cut, construction and composition all effect how a ski performs. A coach or ski shop personnel can help to determine the correct model and size based on the child's weight, height, skiing ability, and skiing discipline (racing, bump skiing, etc.)

Children's skis need to be adequately tuned. Dull edges on hard-packed snow, or skis with bases that are higher than the edges (when the ski is held base upward) will cause skis to slide out. When the edges are higher than the bases, the skis will be difficult to pivot or steer.

Bindings

Binding manufacturers recommend that the complete ski/binding/boot system be inspected by an authorized retailer before each ski season. Also, have bindings checked during the season to ensure appropriate settings as a child grows and becomes a better skier.

Clean snow off boots

"DIN" setting charts are used to determine binding settings. The binding will function better if the setting is not right at the low or high end of the DIN range. The DIN number represents the amount of energy that it takes to release from the binding. Factors that are used to determine a skier's DIN setting are age, weight, boot sole length and skiing ability. It is important for instructors and coaches to familiarize themselves with general binding settings for children in order to identify potential problems.

Young skiers should be taught safety awareness. They must learn to clear all of the dirt, snow or ice off their boots before stepping into their bindings. It is all too easy to overlook this, particularly when a group is in a hurry to get going and skiers are rushed when putting on their skis.

Do not increase DIN settings if a skier releases out of bindings with no apparent cause. Instead, have the ski/binding/boot system checked by an authorized retailer for re-adjustment.

Poles

In general, a child is ready to use ski poles when he or she is able to link wedge turns rhythmically. Until then, ski poles will only be an encumbrance.

To check for the proper pole length, have the child stand in ski boots on a flat surface. Turn the pole over so that the tip is facing up. Have the child grasp the pole right below the basket. The child's forearm should be parallel to the ground with the elbow touching his or her side. If the hand is higher than the elbow, the poles can be cut down to the correct size at a ski shop.

Pole grips with straps are recommended. Plastic strapless grips leave the thumbs more susceptible to injuries and they do not allow for a proper pole swing. Select straps that are easy to put on, adjust, and hold adjustment. To use properly, the hand goes up through the loop of the strap, and then down, gripping the strap and the pole. Fit each strap so that it is snug around your glove when your hand is positioned at the top of the grip. Choose junior poles whenever possible so that the circumference of the pole grip is not too large for the child's hand.

Measuring pole length

Hand positioned at the top of the grip

Goggles

Goggles provide the best eye protection. Sunglasses are more apt to break and they allow potentially damaging rays and wind to enter through the sides of the glasses.

Goggles should have appropriate lenses. On sunny or hazy days use dark lenses for adequate sun protection. On dark, snowy days, use lighter lenses for better visibility. Look for goggles with interchangeable lenses to avoid buying two pairs of goggles. Encourage young children to take care of their goggle lenses so that they stay clean and free of scratches.

Helmets

Ski helmets are recommended for all young skiers. Helmet technology has evolved tremendously in recent years. Its development coincides, in a timely manner, with growth in the ski industry. Groomed slopes and high performance equipment allow skiers to reach high speeds. Obstacles such as signs, trees, snow-making machinery, and lift towers are present. Ski slopes are often crowded, with skiers of different ages, skill levels, and speed capability sharing the same terrain. Even very young children participate in skiing. Considering these factors, it makes good sense to use a helmet. It is especially important for children to wear helmets because they stand the greater risk of injury in a collision with an adult. Children are easily distracted and tend to be less aware than adults regarding changes in upcoming terrain and obstacles. Children's moves can be unpredictable, and it is common for them to dart across a busy slope, perhaps to ski into the woods in search of adventure on a "tree trail." In addition, children who wear helmets have better protection if they are hit by a chairlift when they get on or off the lift.

Necessary features for all-day wear, Slalom, or Giant Slalom helmets include:
(a) a hard plastic shell that is shatter and puncture resistant, providing protection against sharp objects such as ski edges and immovable objects such as rocks and trees.
(b) an expanded polystyrene liner that partially absorbs the shock of an impact
(c) padding for a personalized, snug fit and for warmth
(d) an open ear design that does not disturb hearing or balance
(e) an under-the-chin strap that positions the helmet properly and secures the fit

Optional features include:
(a) a padded rim for extra protection of the face
(b) jaw protection with a removable piece for added protection of the face and teeth
(c) bright colors and graphics for high visibility. Small children become more visible to other skiers when they wear brightly colored helmets.

When it comes to selecting a helmet, correct fit is crucial. To ensure a secure fit, ski helmets should be worn without a hat underneath. The liner of the helmet pro

Helmets (continued)

vides the warmth of a hat. A helmet that is too large will not be as effective in preventing injury because the head can hit the inside of the helmet upon impact. In addition, a helmet that is too large can be too heavy.

Correct helmet size can be determined by measuring the head circumference (in inches or centimeters) and then referring to the manufacturer's sizing chart. Padding can be adjusted or added to ensure a snug and comfortable fit. When an incorrectly sized helmet is excessively padded, protection is compromised, just as excessive padding in too large a ski boot hinders performance. Helmet manufacturers offer sizes ranging from very small helmets for children to extra-large helmets for adults. Various models are designed to meet the needs of all-day wear and the different demands of racing. It is important to use the appropriate model for the situation.

Many people are unaware of the protective values of ski helmets. In other sports that involve speed, obstacles, collisions, and possible contact with stationary objects, protective head gear has evolved to be an accepted part of the athlete's equipment. Football, hockey, bicycling and in-line skating are examples.

Leg Alignment

In a hip-angulated position, the upper body stays relatively vertical, with shoulders level, while the lower body is at a slant to the snow. This is a strong position because it aligns the foot with the knee and the hip in a relatively straight line for support. When the skier's bone structure is aligned, the forces that act on the skis are transmitted through the body in the most efficient manner. As a result, there is less stress on the joints, muscular effort is maximized, and better body position can be achieved. To attain optimum positioning, a skier may need better foot support, angling of the cuff of the boot, or adjustments in the angle at which the boot makes contact with the snow.

Many young skiers need better alignment. Technical inadequacies may be blamed when equipment is really the problem. Werner Schnydrig, Head Junior Coach of the Steamboat Springs Winter Sports Club, extensively evaluates and cants Junior III racers (13 and 14 years old). "I would like to assess skiers of all levels, starting with Junior V's (age 10 years and younger). With young skiers there can be too much play in the equipment, and their strength and skill levels may vary greatly. When I see knee wobble, I'm not sure if it is technique related, strength, or poor alignment, but chances are, it is alignment." Since ski boots break down with use and boot soles get worn, Werner checks his racers often.

In a static position, the ideal alignment of the body in relation to the ski occurs when the ski is flat and the center of the knee mass is slightly to the inside of a line between the hips and the center of the ski boot. Consider a skier who is aligned with the knee to the outside of the center line of the boot on a flat ski. This position is typical of a bow-legged skier. As the skier moves the knee over the center of the boot, edging will occur. When the foot and hip are aligned in the turn, the skier will have more edge angle than is necessary; too much edge. To achieve less edge angle, the skier has to reduce the amount of knee, and/or hip angulation, sacrificing foot to hip alignment. In this circumstance, the outside knee often wobbles in and out as the skier wavers between too much edge angle and too much knee angulation. To improve alignment, add the thick side of the cant to the outside edge of the ski. This helps to re-position the skier's knee to the inside of the center mark of the boot when the ski is flat. After re-alignment, the skier can use knee angulation without over-edging the ski.

In the case of a knock-kneed skier who is aligned with the knee too far to the inside of the center line of the boot, the thick side of the cant should be added to the inside edge of the ski. This will bring the knee in a position that is about one centimeter to the inside of the center line of the boot. When the knee is too far inside, the ski remains flat while knee and/or hip angles already occur. This skier has to move extremely to the inside of the turn or tuck one knee behind the other in order to get enough edge to grip the snow. In this circumstance, the outside ski often rails; continues on a straight course without turning. When the skier's alignment is corrected with canting, the skier can use knee angulation and achieve sufficient edge angle.

Body/ski alignment can be effected by the position of

the foot in the boot. An unsupported or fatigued foot can alter knee alignment. The upper cuff of the boot can negatively affect alignment when it does not correspond with the curvature of the lower leg. Individual body characteristics, such as different leg lengths and femoral rotation, also effect alignment.

Improved structural alignment can be attained through a three step process:
  (1) support the foot with an orthotic device or molded foot-bed
  (2) adjust the angle of the upper cuff to correspond with the angle of the lower leg
  (3) cant, if necessary, to achieve optimum knee alignment between the boot and the hip

Leg alignment will be different for a non-supported foot (the arch flattens and the foot can tip inward) compared to a supported foot. When the foot is supported, it stays in a strong position and does not flatten when the boot is buckled. It is also important for the boot to be the correct size in order to provide good support. An arch support, custom-molded foot-bed, or orthotic device can be added to, or replace the insole, depending on the amount of support that is best for each person. Besides helping to align the body effectively, personalized insoles can make your boots more comfortable. Boot fitting specialists at retail stores can help to access your needs.

After the foot is sufficiently supported, adjust the upper cuff of the boot so that the lower leg is centered in the cuff. To find the centered position, remove the liner, place the foot-bed in the boot shell and adjust the cuff allowing equal space on either side of the leg. After this adjustment is made, the angle of the boot cuff will not force the lower leg into an unnatural position. Since not all junior boots have cant adjustments, skier's that have significant lower leg curvature should select a junior boot that does adjust. If this is not possible, have the adjustment made by canting under the binding.

The angle at which the boot makes contact with the ski is altered with the use of wedges, or *cants*. Typically, this is accomplished by placing cants under the bindings. Some racers have the soles of their boots planed or sanded to achieve the appropriate angle. Material is then added to the top of the toe and heel to return the thickness to DIN specifications. This is an expensive process and it is not always an available option. Some

Cant under binding

racers choose to have their boot soles altered rather than canting many pairs of skis. This also allows them to switch their right and left skis in order to have "new" inside edges for racing.

To determine if, and to what extent cants are necessary, follow these steps:

   (a) stand in boots (buckled for skiing) and skis on a flat floor
   (b) stand in a balanced position with joints flexed and eyes looking ahead
   (c) place skis in a parallel position
   (d) the distance the skis are apart should be close to hip width. Young skier's hips are so narrow that a stance with skis one to two inches apart is typically appropriate.
   (e) flatten skis against the floor
   (f) mark a line on the knee cap to indicate the center of the knee mass
   (g) hang a plumb bob (string with a pointed weight) from this mark
   (h) mark a line on the boot toe where the plumb bob points
   (i) use strips of duct tape under the inside or outside edge of the ski to position the point of the plumb bob one centimeter to the inside (toward the big toe) of the center line on the boot
   (j) measure the thickness of the duct tape to determine how thick the cant should be
   (k) work with a good boot fitter who is an alignment specialist at a retail store in order to add cants under the binding. The *Lange* ski boot company has developed a device that is available in many ski shops for the purpose of making alignment assessments.

AFTERWORD

Alan Schönberger

The Turning Point Ski Foundation is a non-profit organization that develops and publishes educational material to help young skiers achieve their goals. Books, such as *Technical Skills for Alpine Skiing*, are designed to better skiers' experiences as they strive for excellence.

Technical Skills for Alpine Skiing began as a project for the US Ski Coaches Association. Ellen was asked to provide a program, based on well-rounded skiing fundamentals, that would provide a strong technical foundation for future US Ski Team racers. Her original work, entitled the *Alpine Skills Achievement Manual*, provided a wealth of exercises and progressions that were adeptly organized to ensure skill development. *Technical Skills for Alpine Skiing* further develops the material contained in the original manual.

For her writings, Ellen has drawn from her extensive and impressive background as both a junior and an international competitor. Her skiing career began in 1968 as a member of the *Jiminy Peak Junior Demonstration Team* in Massachusetts. The program emphasized perfecting fundamental skills which proved to provide a strong technical base and theme for her later accomplishments. The demonstration team evolved into a junior freestyle team, preparing Ellen to become a world-class competitor on the professional freestyle tour in 1974. Ellen placed second overall in the 1975 *Freestyle World Championships* and is the only person to ever win an aerial, ballet, mogul and combined event all in the same year. Never losing sight of the impact of her junior team experiences, Ellen directed her education to teaching and coaching. She was a member of the *Professional Ski Instructors of America National Demonstration Team* from 1980 to 1988 and a member of two U.S. Interski Teams.

During this time, Ellen was the head coach for the Winter Park, Colorado junior ski team. Many Junior Olympic champions emerged from her program. Ellen worked closely with one coach, Werner Schnydrig, discussing observations, comparing notes and sharing ideals. When Werner left Winter Park to direct the junior program at Steamboat Springs, he provided a testing ground for the material in the *Alpine Skills Achievement Manual*. Many of the young demonstrators that you see in this book are from Werner's program. They were raised on the exercises and progressions that are contained in this book. This past winter, ten-year-olds, Cassidy Kurtz and Tony Cesolini won the *Rocky Mountain Junior V Championships*. Brett Buckles and David Lamb qualified for the *Rocky Mountain Honorary Junior III Team* (13–14 year-olds) with their Junior Olympic results at age thirteen.

As the photographer, my challenge was to reveal the beaurty of skiing through images of the child athlete–to capture ten-year-old World Cup moments. With this book, you have the opportunity to develop champion skiers. But more importantly, you can encourage the development of qualities such as personal fortitude, confidence in the face of challenge, and the desire to strive for excellence. Through skiing, children can experience the joy of movement, the thrill of meeting challenges and the inexpressible wonder of success. We invite you to share our commitment toward enriching the lives of young people through the sport of skiing.

The Mountain Playground

New snow had fallen the night before. My group gathered around me before the mountain was awakened by crowds of powder seekers. In the early morning light, eager eyes shined through goggles on faces hidden under hats and zipped-up collars. Greetings were whispered or nodded, no one daring to disturb the quiet morning and break the spell of anticipation.

"Let's go to the playground!" spoke a little voice belonging to Brett, the youngest of the group. "You know," he continued, "the place off the side of the Meadows. My mountain playground."

The slope he referred to fell away from the edge of the Meadows, gradually disappearing into the woods below. A fire had claimed much of the hillside but had left fallen logs amongst tree stumps and boulders. On this day, the regrowth of small pine trees was covered with new snow and only the shapes of the obstructions were visible. The wind had blown the night before, sculpting the snow into a white world of snow drifts, rolls, ridges, dips and jumps.

The deep snow muffled the sounds of skiing as we approached the Meadows. I remember how the silence burst into laughter and shouts of delight as Brett led the way into the playground. From the Meadow's edge, I viewed the mountain from a new perspective.

New snow had fallen the night before on another occasion: Members of the PSIA Demonstration Team gathered around their coach in anticipation of skiing for a film. As a team member, I spoke of the mountain in the way that Brett had enlightened me. From my comments, the film became entitled, "The Mountain Playground." It emphasized the application of technique to the challenges of the terrain, of the mountain.

This led to national focus, and the theme was introduced internationally at Interski in 1987. The presentation by the Professional Ski Instructors of America began with, "The purpose of our workshop is to demonstrate how the student's enjoyment of the mountain playground is enhanced by developing new movement possibilities and strategies." All because of the words spoken by a six-year-old on a wintry day.

The printing of this book was made possible through generous contributions from *Dynastar* skis, *Lange* boots, *Kerma* poles, *MPH Associates, Inc.* (distributor of *Boeri* helmets), *Marker* bindings, *Bolle* goggles, *Arapahoe Basin Resort*, and the *Turning Point Ski Foundation.* In addition, grants were provided by the *PSIA–Central* division's *Education Foundation* and *PSIA–Rocky Mountain* division's *Education Foundation.* Clothing was provided by *Schure Sports U.S.A. Inc.* (distributor of *Phenix* skiwear) and the *Moriarty Hat & Sweater Company.*

EQUIPMENT INFORMATION

The "demonstration team" for *Technical Skills for Alpine Skiing* used equipment from the following companies. To learn more about their products, information can be obtained by contacting the companies directly.

Dynastar, Lange, Kerma
P.O. Box 25, Hercules Drive
Colchester, VT 05446-0025
Phone: 802.655.2400 Fax: 802.655.4329

Boeri Ski and Snowboard Helmets
MPH Associates, Inc.
PO Box 567
Norwood, MA 02062

Marker USA
PO Box 26548
Salt Lake City, UT 84126
Phone: 801.972.2100 Fax: 801.973.7241

Bolle America, Inc.
3890 Elm Street
Denver, CO 80207
Phone: 303.321.4300 Fax: 303.321.6952

Phenix
Schure Sports U.S.A. Inc.
161 Deerhide Crescent, Unit 9A
Weston, Ontario
M9M 2Z2
Canada
Phone: 416.741.2119 Fax: 416.741.2388

Moriarty Hat & Sweater Co.
112 Main Street, Box 1117
Stowe, VT 05672
Phone: 802.253.4052

ORDERING INFORMATION

To order the following books, please send your name, address, and cost of book(s) plus $3.00 postage to:

Turning Point Ski Foundation
PO Box 943
Edwards, CO 81632
puppet@vailnet.org

Technical Skills for Alpine Skiing
Price $15.95

Race Skills for Alpine Skiing
Price $14.95

"This book presents the most well-rounded approach to ski racing that I have seen. The book is systematic, logical, and clear. Using very specific, easily understood exercises, Foster enlivens highly complex subject matter. She has an impressive ability to isolate the key skills and ingredients in a clear, concise manner. It is essential reading for coaches, instructors and developing athletes."
—Mike Porter
    Director, Vail/Beaver Creek Ski School
    Head Coach, PSIA National Demonstration Team

Conditioning Skills for Alpine Skiing
Price $11.95

"This book takes a fun approach to the physical development of young skiers. It represents the latest information about the physical conditioning of pre- and post-adolescent athletes. This information will make a significant impact on the preparation of young skiers for a sport in which they can participate throughout their entire life time."
—Charles J. Dillman, Ph.D.
    Executive Director,
    Steadman • Hawkins Sports Medicine Foundation

NOTES